Staying

*A Multi-Generational Memoir
of Rescue and Restoration*

By William Sanders

Heart Quest Publishing

ISBN-10: 0692452850

ISBN-13: 978-0-692-45285-1

Cover Design by Laura Sanders

Published in Acworth, Georgia, by Heart Quest Publishing

www.william-sanders.com

"William Sanders' *Staying* is a beautiful account of how our God brings good out of bad. It is intimate, vulnerable and honest. You will see yourself somewhere in William's story, and more importantly, you will get a glimpse of God's heart toward William, and thus, His heart toward us. It is a fantastic read." – **Mac Powell,** *Lead Singer, Third Day*

"Everybody has a story – some more fascinating than others. As I read the story of William Sanders, I was literally hooked from the first page. This is a beautiful tale of restoration, which I think is the kind of story closest to the heart of God." – **Jeff Foxworthy,** *Comedian and Bestselling Author*

"The unfathomable betrayal and riveting rescue of this lost boy reveals a father who relentlessly pursues his children no matter the cost. William's journey from a life of fleeing to staying is our story, too. For we are sons and daughters of a Father who refuses to leave us as spiritual orphans but, as the Great Stayer, transforms us through the scars of our story into our truer selves." – **Allen Arnold,** *Director of Content & Resources, Ransomed Heart Ministries*

"Every father should read *Staying*. William Sanders' story of childhood abandonment and abduction would have been a gritty, well-told story on its own. But reading how God used William's past to prepare him to be a father and a stayer for a daughter who desperately needed what he had to offer is a beautiful reminder of how God works all things together for good."
– **Mark Schlabach,** *Co-Author of* Called to Coach: Reflections on Life, Faith, and Football *with Former Florida State Football Coach Bobby Bowden and Co-Author of* The Duck Commander Family: How Faith, Family and Ducks Built a Dynasty

"William Sanders wants us to know that God is faithful and works to bring about good from even the worst of life's circumstances. William's own life is a story of God's rescue, grace and redemption. He writes in an original and inspiring way. Your heart will long to believe what William Sanders believes because of the freedom and ultimate joy it has brought him."
– **Andrew Farley,** *Bestselling Author of* The Naked Gospel, God Without Religion, *and* Relaxing With God; *Host, Andrew Farley LIVE on Sirius XM*

"I found *Staying* to be an excellent read. It was highly personal and gripping. I loved seeing 40 years of God moving in William's life to bring him to the perfect place at the perfect time. William tells his story beautifully. You won't be disappointed."
– **Frank Page,** *Former President, Southern Baptist Convention*

This book is for you, Dad.

Acknowledgments

The list of those deserving my gratitude is long. Many will have to settle for me thanking them in person, or in an email.

To Jane, Rachel and Laura, you are my life. Thanks for loving me well.

To Stan, my best friend for 35 years, no one loves you like I do. And I know no one loves me like you do. Thanks for teaching me how to say things like that to another man.

To John Lynch, thank you for expanding my dependence on grace and teaching me to sell out to it, and to Pastor Craig Bowler for caring about my story.

Thanks to the marvelous manuscript editor Mick Silva. Every writer needs a great editor. You can borrow him, but bring him back like you found him. And thanks to Allen Arnold, for your kind advice and belief in my story. Thanks to Laura Sanders for her brilliant creative services.

Thank you to my sisters, Cindy Adams and Amy Park, and my mom, Lucy Sanders, for being just whacky enough to write about. Cindy, this is our story. Thanks for letting me write it.

Lastly, thank you, Dad. You fathered me well. And you were, and still are, heroic to your family.

The story here is true. Only a few names have been changed.

Contents

Foreword

I've known William Sanders for a long time. But I didn't know he could pull this off – to write so eloquently and honestly of that devastating season when he and his sister were stolen. And he did it all without dodging the "Where was God?" questions, or tying everything together into a sanitized, sloganized, religious, morality play.

Many of us can no longer endure much of what passes for a "testimony." For in their stated goal of trying to build up our trust in God, they can form a redaction of something false, syrupy and disingenuous – an always clearly happy ending, which works neatly into a twenty-minute, ironclad sermonette.

Life does not usually work that way. God does not usually work that way. And to force His intention and reworking of evil into quickly explainable, smugly controverted, victory speeches, actually discourages my faith. Because I can't so easily explain what God has been doing in my life.

But every now and then you find a writer who trusts God is big enough to be comfortable with the entire story, without doing injustice to either.

Through painful, risky questioning, the writer ends up – in front of the reader – trusting the Author. The story can be gruff and the writer more gruff. But there is a winsome delightfulness in authentic gruff when it's mixed with tenderness and well-crafted humor. It all gives me permission to explore my own unresolved pain, despair and untied threads of reality.

This is the God I am able to trust when the unthinkable lands at my doorstep.

Staying is such a story. In a carefully chronicled narrative only a skilled journalist can paint, William captures innocence, honesty and somehow even laughter from his unique vantage point as the deeply caring brother of a taken sister and stolen childhood.

William is not just telling a family story, he is telling our story with God. For each of us have experienced, from childhood all through adulthood, countless seasons appearing to make almost no sense at all. Some of us run from God, some of us learn to ignore Him. Some of us – almost in spite of ourselves – allow Him to love us in the deepest parts of our being.

William captures our story, the one where we are trying to make sense of a God who loves us enough to eventually redeem our life experiences without always completely explaining how. You are in for honest life, honestly told, honestly healed.

Did I mention he is my friend? And he has been this for me – The Great Stayer.

– **John Lynch**, co-author of *True Faced* and *The Cure;* author, *On My Worst Day*

Preface

I have no memory of the events from my first five years of life.

After 40 years of subtly convincing me I didn't need to know what happened to me as a little boy – mainly by avoiding the conversation completely – Dad changed his mind.

Turns out, all I had to do was ask.

After 40 years of never revisiting the pain we'd all endured, Dad shifted. "Do I like to think about it or talk about it?" my dad said to my sister Cindy on Jan. 6, 2014. "No. But for Bill, I will." Translation: For his son, he'd put aside embarrassment, pride, masculinity and concern about what others might think.

This is the kind of dad I have. So I suppose I shouldn't be surprised at his willingness to forsake what he thought was best to do what I needed. He did it 40 years ago, and he's done it countless times since.

But what can I say? I'm a slow learner. Maybe a doubter?

Regardless, 24 hours later, I sit in my upstairs den, in the dark of an early winter evening preparing myself to hear the events of my childhood I know next to nothing about. It's 6 o'clock, and the glare from my computer screen and the outside street light are the only things keeping me from being in total darkness.

Six o'clock means Dad is on his second Scotch of the evening. I had calculated that in advance and decided that one Scotch down and the next one there for the sipping should be just about right for this kind of talk, even though we'd never had *this* kind of talk.

But my house is too quiet. Jane isn't home from work yet, and my two daughters are gone, too – one rehearsing for her school play, the other out living her life. I've never liked the kind of dead silence that lets you hear your heart beating. And mine was beating a little louder than normal.

I turn the television on, which adds some background light, but not much. I lower the volume to a couple notches above mute and sit down in my most comfortable chair, rest my feet on the ottoman and call my dad.

I'm going to try hard to hide the fact that I'm largely undone by the sacrificial love he's showing me here. I hold back because that's what we do. We respect silence so as to not cause the other pain or worry. This conversation neither of us thought we'd ever have has been decades in the making. So I know downplaying it would be a token gesture that would only add to the discomfort. We both know the immense import of the next hour or so. And what's more, we know the other one knows, as well.

"Hey, Dad."

"Hey, Sport."

For all of my adult life, three or four times a week, phone calls, usually initiated by Dad, would start with the enthusiastic, "Hey Sport!" as if he hadn't talked to me in months. It's a sweet, genuine greeting that I've always taken for granted, but hope to never again.

This time though, it's weighty and serious.

"I'll tell you whatever you want to know," he says. "I'll tell you everything. And I want you to write it."

When I began collecting bits of evidence a couple of months earlier, my assumption was that my story would be built around questions, some of which I would learn answers to by digging through records or talking with a few people on the periphery who might still have some recollection of what happened in the early 1970s. I was certain, though, that many questions would remain unanswered.

In fact, up until Dad said yes, up until I'd mustered the courage to ask him, I'd assumed, "I don't know and I probably never will," would be the most frequent refrain in this quick story.

Cindy and I had talked about the events of our childhood many times over the years. Almost always, it ended at the void in our knowledge of what really happened. It was frustrating, but we were willing to learn to live with it. Or without it, I suppose.

We didn't ask questions of my dad for two reasons: First, we'd been brought up to sweep things well under the rug and pretend. The plausible deniability act, putting on a face and smiling, that's what I knew from as early on as I can remember. So much so, I started believing that this lumpy rug beneath me was fashionable, comfortable and safe, even as it was getting bulkier.

Secondly, we honored our father and that meant honoring his clear desire not to talk about it. He'd earned that right as far as we were concerned. While he had not been a flawless father to either of us, he'd been a heroic one, and an admirable one and a good one. And he still is.

Both of those reasons were sufficient for me and for Cindy for decades.

But I've just come out of a horrifying few years dealing with my older daughter's debilitating anxiety. During that hyper-focused time, worrying about what made me *me* –and thus, what made Rachel *Rachel* – was impossible.

And now that my life's state of constant crisis has passed, the slow simmering desire to know my story is now boiling into a full-blown urgency. I'm deciding, for myself and for all of us, the cover-ups are pretending are no longer enough. Too much has happened, too much is roiling inside of me to ignore it any longer. I draw a line in the sand and embrace the belief that whatever the truth is, it will set me free. And Rachel free. And Dad and Cindy, as well.

I know my dad will face things that will be difficult to accept. In fact, it's the only thing that's giving me a minute's pause this time and the primary reason I have been silent all this time. I'd be lying if I said it was the only reason though. I knew, too, that I'd probably learn things that would be easier to not know.

But I wonder: What if the probing and talking could bring us closer through the pain? Would that bring evidence of a radical grace none of us has ever known in such fullness? Could we experience such a thing together? I have to admit, that kind of grace and wonder intrigues me. And maybe the hope of it will spur me on a little bit, when the journey becomes so dark over the eerie months of coming to terms with my story.

As a storytelling journalist for daily newspapers for two decades, I was at my best when I could look my subject in the eye and say: "I will handle your story with care." Dozens of times over the years, I asked families to share hard, painful truths with me so I could write them for hundreds of thousands of people to read. I'd ask the subjects to be vulnerable, to unzip the chest and bare their soul.

I couldn't do this early in my career because I didn't know how to talk that way, and more importantly, I wasn't sure I could handle their story with the level of care they deserved.

Talking that way, with compassionate confidence, is hard. And it can't be faked. You have to mean it – all of it. Many people don't know how to talk about things that really matter. That, though, is our common burden. As a journalist, it caused me to back away from stories that required seeking, demanding, that level of intimacy for years.

But by the time I reached my pinnacle as a newspaper reporter, I could talk the talk and walk the walk with complete sincerity. And that's the only reason I can do that now with Cindy's story and with Dad's.

Part of me, maybe the noble-striving part, was initially convinced this was going to be Cindy's story more than mine. She was the one who'd been through the worst, in my mind. But then I thought, no, it was going to be my dad's story. I'd honor him that way, because whatever's good in me is there by my father's blessing, a treasure not every boy can claim.

I convinced myself I could tell this story and keep myself relatively hidden, safe in the background, narrating what was happening all around me. But how could I expect to know the depths of *their* stories? And wouldn't that really be me refusing to be vulnerable and calling it a selfless sacrifice?

For the first time – and once and for all – I would have to lay claim to whatever came during my search and take ownership of it.

This is my story.

Chapter 1 – The Journey

"And you will be given a new name by the LORD's own mouth." – Isaiah 62:2

"You actually believe anyone up there cares about you? – The Deceiver

L ying in bed, praying for the umpteenth time for God to show up and be the God his word says he is, I wrestle with what my next prayer will be, even though I am not at all sure it matters. While I haven't lost faith that there is a God, and that Jesus came to save me, as well as the world, right now, that means nothing to me.

I am bled dry of the kind of faith that once had me convinced that my prayers mattered to God.

"Heal Rachel; don't heal Rachel, I don't care. You decide."

Of course, I care. But out of an exhausted frustration, those three words are part of my short, angry prayer.

That prayer barely edges out this one: "Let my daughter die. Figure out a painless, quick way to bring her home to you, and out of this hell we are living. And, oh by the way God, I'm fine with you taking me, too."

Countless times, I had prayed for Jesus to come back and take us all out of this mess of a life we were living. But that kind of prayer, and a "Let-her-die" prayer are hardly in the same realm.

Rachel's emotional and anxiety-ridden spiral, a several-year-long ride, has taken me to the emotional depths of hopelessness. Short of heaven, I see no hope.

Maybe others could forget their child's daily angst and nightly trauma and simply pack their bags and move out, maybe give the single-life a crack again. I know I cannot leave; I don't have the capacity to do it. My heart is so invested in Rachel's day-to-day, hour-by-hour emotional state, that leaving would be harder for me than staying.

How could that even be, when staying is draining every bit of hope, faith and energy out of my body? Simple. Her fleeting hours of joy and rest and calm – the times when I see her playing with Megan or Caroline in the den or whenever she answers "good" to my relentless question of "how are you feeling?" – feed me like nothing else. Healthy or not, I'm living for those morsels of manna.

Plus, I believe if I leave, my heart would stop being relevant to me. And not too long after that, it might stop beating altogether, because who wants to live life with an irrelevant heart?

And without the grace and intervention of God, I believe me leaving might just kill Rachel, too. Healthy or not, I was her rock, her earthly picture of an all-loving God. You've heard before that you might be the only Jesus someone sees? I was Christ in Bill Sanders, and although Rachel was seeing a messed-up and imperfect outer shell, she was somehow seeing through that to the flawless image of the Almighty that lives within me.

I am coming to terms with the fact that, like it or not, I am in this for the long haul.

The concept of staying – staying in the arena, staying present, staying in the battle for my heart and Rachel's – had never entered my head or heart when the living was routine, or easy or pleasant. But no one gets the easy-living life for long. Decay takes over. Cancer sprouts. An affair tears into a marriage. A car crash leaves your spouse paralyzed. It's then that staying, or leaving, becomes deliberate.

For me, with the living anything but easy and pleasant, I'm trapped in a harsh reality: I don't want to stay; I cannot leave.

What other way out is there then? If I can't just walk away from my family, maybe divorce my wife, dull it all with Maker's Mark and become a deadbeat dad, what other escape is there? Oh, there is another way out. A permanent one. Again, thanks to the grace of God, that thought never lands in my brain for more than a second or two. But every stinking day and every sleep-interrupted night, I ache to be out of this pain and to go to my eternal home where I belong. Much more so, I ache for Rachel to be there.

Sanity and grace cause me to know that killing myself would do no one any good. Even in my worst pain, or while watching Rachel in her worst pain, my sense of duty and the understanding of the trauma that it would do to my family keep that thought at bay.

But I am so unable to see God's bigger picture, and instead am so hyper-focused on my here and now and what Rachel's darkness is doing to her and to me, I cannot trust the plans He has to prosper us and love us through these times. Or maybe I'm choosing not to trust them. Either way, I don't want Rachel to live this way. I don't want her to have to stay in this bloodthirsty arena.

Before uttering what I call my angry prayer of release, I lie in bed and envision her in Jesus' arms. I let myself think I could come to terms with this scenario, Rachel out of her crippling pain and me off the hook from having to fix her. I'd grieve. I'd bury the majority of my heart with her body. I'd never love the same way again. I'd be a shattered shell of the husband Jane deserved and the father Laura deserved. But in the visions, those all were tradeoffs I was willing to make. Damn the collateral damage.

In this scenario, I don't think about Jane. Or Laura. Or the thousands who will never know her. In this dark daydream, I'm taking on her pain, knowing I would never be rid of it. But she'd be in heaven, never to be near it.

This should not need to be said, but it probably does. I never thought of a way to usher Rachel out of her pain and into God's arms. Again, sanity and grace.

Finally, after begging, fasting, crying, enlisting the best prayer warriors I knew, God shows up, but it's in a way that makes no sense to me, at least not at first. He doesn't show up to put his hand on Rachel and take away the life-sucking anxieties that rule her life. That's what I had been waiting on and what would have made sense to me. Instead, He shows up to give me a new name, and to take me on a 40-year journey back in time to show why He is giving me this name.

And because He loves me, and because He knows I'm running on empty, God begins to give me the first glimpse of my life from a heavenly perspective.

I'm lying on Rachel's floor at the foot of her bed. About 15 minutes earlier, I'd thought she was asleep and I'd tried to tiptoe out of her room and back to my bedroom, but she woke up, startled at the sound of a slightly creaky floor. I'm not sure she ever really goes to sleep and instead always tinkers on the edge of consciousness and sleep, to afraid to allow herself to not be on guard.

"I'm here," I tell her. "I'll stay until you are asleep."

"And then some?"

"Yes, and then some."

Her restless legs rattle beneath the sheets, and I do the only thing there is to do when laying silently on a little girl's floor. I pray.

"Please God, let this be the night. Give her rest. Give me rest. Psalms says you give your beloved rest. We are your beloved. Please God, give us rest. I don't want to stay here all night."

"You are the Great Stayer," God whispered to me.

"The Great What? What does that even mean? What's that supposed to do for me? How's that any help for Rachel? You show up to give me a new name and kind of a lame one at that? Do you not see what is going on here, that Rachel's legs are kicking, her mind racing and I'm laying on her floor for the millionth night in a row?"

These are the questions I ask because I have not guarded my heart above all else, and it had been under a brutal, relentless assault. The thief had come. And he had stolen, he had killed and he had destroyed.

Tenderly, with no condemnation or frustration, He answers.

"I do see, always. Before it happens, I see. And I weep with you and with Rachel. You don't see everything now. You won't see how it is all tied together for good on this side of eternity. But I'm here, today, right now, to show you some of it, and give you a new perspective on how and why you were made for this. It's in your DNA because I sewed it together myself."

Taking this 40,000-foot panoramic view of my life, I am reminded of the times of my own tremendous hurt as a child, the times I was abandoned and many, many desperate pleas for God. But I also see glimpses of an innocence that I presumed was lost. I see times of hope and faithfulness and great love. And I get my truest sense yet of whom God is. And how little I understand His ways.

The journey begins with me being six years old. And I'm in a bad way.

God said:

I'm glad you are telling your story, our story

Chapter 2 – Taken

"God, investigate my life; get all the facts firsthand." – Psalms 139:1 (The Message)

"Careful what you ask for." – The Deceiver

August 1971

It is my first memory of attempting to control an uncontrollable situation. I have just turned six years old, and I'm not yet good at controlling much of anything, particularly something that is rocking my fragile heart and scaring me in a way that I'd never known.

I don't remember any specifics about life before this day, August 5, 1971. Actually, I don't even remember how this day started, or exactly how I had found myself in the backseat of this car, sitting next to my sister Cindy, who is about to turn nine years old, and who is far too young for what is about to be asked of her.

"Let us go home and pack something," I said to my mom, who had disappeared until today almost a year earlier. "Or we can do this another time. Just take us back home and we'll figure it out from there."

Those may not have been my exact words, but tearfully, that is the exact case I'm making for why Cindy and I should not be kidnapped. Of course, I have not rehearsed for such a situation, so I'm neither convincing nor effective. It's also the first time I remember failing.

"Oh no, Bill. We ARE going to the airport and we ARE going to Tampa. Today. Now," said Charlotte, from the driver's seat, with her mother, a weak, small browbeaten woman sitting next in the passenger seat next to her.

It takes 45 minutes to drive from Nana and Pops' house to the Atlanta airport. Cindy and I had lived with my grandparents and my dad now. About six months ago, while Dad was at work one day, my mom had dropped us off at a neighbor's house one morning and left. She'd made the same drive to the same airport all alone, gotten on the same plane to the same city and out of our lives for what all I knew would be forever.

This was the first time I'd seen her since.

Now she's driving me away from whatever semblance of security and innocence I had been clinging to the last half year. I'd been abandoned way too recently to have the level of security and innocence a little boy should have.

But with every passing mile on Interstate 75 and then Interstate 85, and then with the 500 miles through the air, we're getting so far away I'm not at all sure that I'll ever be able to fully find my way back. Mommy is taking us headfirst into a lifetime of fear with the windows rolled down.

This is not an ugly custody squabble playing out. It is not a case of a good mother who would go to any extreme to be with her kids, even if it meant skirting the rules or the laws. Of course I couldn't verbalize it then, but on some level I know, even at this tender age, that the backseat of this car traveling down the highway is ground zero in a battle of good versus evil.

This is more akin to abduction by a stranger. I recognize this woman as my mom, but I don't really know her. I certainly don't know what she is capable of and I don't have a single memory of her ever acting motherly.

So while I probably don't even know what kidnapping means, I know with as much certainty as a 6-year-old boy can have that I am in trouble. There is no way Nana and Pop, or especially Dad, would be OK with this. And neither am I.

I cry on the way to Atlanta's Hartsfield International Airport. Cindy does not. Instead, she is doing what the older sibling is supposed to do in the midst of chaos and crisis. She is trying to comfort me.

"It's gonna be fine, Bill," she says, at first talking loud enough for Charlotte to hear. "We'll get on an airplane, go to Florida and be home before the weekend is over."

Then, quieter, almost whispering and only for me to hear, she says it again.

"We'll be OK. It's our mom. We'll be OK."

This is Cindy's first crack at telling a lie for the sole purpose of making someone else feel hopeful. And like my first attempt at controlling a situation, it's not working.

"We'll get there and you'll see that it's not so bad," the woman formerly known as my mom says. I'm not sure if she quit being mom when she first left us, or whether it was sometime over the ensuing six months, or if it happened 20 minutes ago. . "We're calling your Nana to tell her the plans. She won't mind. Neither will your dad.

"Liar," I think to myself but don't dare say out loud. For that one moment, I was equal parts scared for myself and mad that she would say that and expect us to believe it.

"We're staying with Mary Ellen at her apartment. You remember Mary Ellen. She adores you and Cindy. And there's a beach in Tampa."

Mary Ellen. I'm no longer equal parts mad and scared. I'm 100 percent scared again.

"Can we go back home first?" I asked.

"No, we've got to get to the airport."

"When are we coming back home?"

"We'll see."

Charlotte's mother, "Gan" to Cindy and me, keeps quiet.

As we walk through the Atlanta airport, I think about finding a policeman and running to him. But I don't. That takes courage, and right now, for the first time, I can tell that I don't have it.

We make our way through the airport terminal without a scene. We get on a plane and two hours later, we are in Tampa. Tampa might as well have been Tokyo. Or Mars. It's that distant and unknown to me.

The woman formerly known as my mom, Charlotte, is beauty queen material with blonde hair and a charming first look. As promised, this beauty queen drives us straight to Mary Ellen's apartment. Mary Ellen is a short, stumpy, frizzy-haired woman, with Brillo-like hair, and is not a beauty queen in anyone's pageant. I think she is somewhat familiar to me, which is to say I recognize her, but not much more. But she will become a major player in our story. And despite what my mom had just told us, she certainly doesn't adore Cindy or me.

Also as promised, Gan calls Nana.

Of course I didn't hear the call, but I've been told it was short: "Era, Charlotte has taken the kids to Tampa. They belong with their mother."

What kind of grandmother aids and abets is such a bold abduction? By all accounts, she's neither a bad person nor a strong one. Perhaps she's under duress herself. Maybe she's seen enough in her own daughter to not want on her bad side.

Nana holds it together, at least for now, and calls the hotel where Dad is staying in Greensboro, N.C., for a business trip.

"Billy…Charlotte has kidnapped the kids," Nana said. "They're headed to Tampa. I just got a call from Alice Burns."

What's a dad do with that kind of phone call? Fall to pieces? Not yet. Follow his instincts? Yep. And for a father, that almost always means rolling into action – immediately.

Heartbroken, scared and erratic, Dad drives to Charlotte, N.C., and catches a flight to Tampa. He asks Nana and Pop to leave their Atlanta home and make the nine-hour drive to Tampa.

No one knows exactly what their assignment will be once they get to Tampa. They'll worry about that once they are all en route.

All of this is happening on a Thursday, I think, though I can't swear to it.

Our jail cell in Tampa is a bedroom with two twin beds. The first night we are there, Cindy and I are awake at midnight, watching the Tonight Show with Johnny Carson on the small black-and-white TV. Six-year-olds don't really get into The Tonight Show, but it's what's on, and it's providing some background noise and some needed distraction. I'm sleepy but afraid to go to sleep.

"Isn't it cool that we get to stay up so far past our bedtime?" Cindy asked. "We're watching Johnny Carson. We never get to watch Johnny Carson. We're going to be OK, you know. I promise.

Cindy doesn't believe that, mind you. But what she believes isn't important at the moment. Someone has to take care of me. So it is going to be an eight-year-old – but at least it is an eight-year-old who is going to be nine in 11 days. And at least she loves me, and sometimes even likes me.

"Go to sleep," she said. "I'll talk to you until you fall asleep. And I'll be here when you wake up. And we'll go back home soon, maybe Sunday."

The next thing I remember, it's Sunday morning. Friday and Saturday may have been unremarkable, but I don't recall. But on this Sunday morning, Cindy wakes up not feeling well, probably an emotional wreck from the events of the past few days.

"Stay home with Mary Ellen," Charlotte told Cindy. "Get dressed, Bill. We're going to church."

In what bizarre world does the kidnapper take the kid to church? But then again, nothing about this scheme was playing out in an expected way.

Mary Ellen smokes all day and drinks a good bit of it. She is scary looking and with her gravely and gruff voice, is scary sounding. She looks disheveled and old, much older than 31, which is what she is. This is going to be Cindy's babysitter. But for now, that is Cindy's cross to bear. I had been told to get dressed, and that's exactly what I was going to do. I figure a woman capable of whatever it is she is doing isn't one to be disobeyed.

So with Cindy still in bed, I get dressed, which means the same clothes I'd been wearing for three days.

It had been raining that morning, as we walked into Hyde Park United Methodist Church, I don't remember a thing about the service or what the church looked like on the inside.

I don't remember praying at church that morning. I can't imagine I'd have needed to though. If God wasn't already at work on behalf of one of His children, then I'm not sure what I could have said to convince Him. Again, I didn't have those skills anyway. I was at the mercy of others, dependent on grace, even though I didn't yet know what the word meant.

I hadn't for a second questioned that I'd been wrongfully taken from my home. God didn't need me to tell Him my story, lay out the desperation of my situation. He knew.

I vividly remember the parking lot though, and walking through it after church. The dark clouds that had escorted us that morning have broken and the sun is out.,

I get into the front passenger seat, and because it is humid, I roll down the window the instant the door shuts.

I never saw him coming.

Between the moment in which I got into the car and when Charlotte is able to pull out, a pair of arms reaches through the open window, grabs me, and yanks me out of the car.

People in the parking lot are screaming as they walk out of church. Women use their umbrellas to beat my savior upside his head.

"Someone call the police!" a woman was yelling.

"Stop that man!" screams another, while grabbing at me.

A large, green Chrysler, which is the most familiar thing I have seen the last 72 hours, is parked off to the side, the engine running, the nose pointed toward the parking lot exit.

I came out one car through a window, and moments later I am being shoved through the door and onto the floorboard of another car. Then the man jumps into the driver's seat and speeds away.

"Stay down," I am told. "Don't let anyone see you. The police will be looking for us."

Things aren't always as they seem.

Everyone in that church parking lot were certain they had just seen a kidnapping. Of course, the real one was 72 hours earlier.

What they were seeing was a rescue, a dangerous, selfless act that could have left him arrested, assaulted, or worse. The odds that such a reckless, seemingly random mission would succeed, even if performed by a trained private investigator or, heck, for that matter a Special Forces Op, had to be close to zero.

The fact that it is my 61-year-old paternal grandfather pulling this off requires God's careful orchestration. Success for him and my grandmother, his accomplice waiting in the Chrysler, looks like this:

– They'd have to hope the intel they had gotten that Charlotte had taken us to church was accurate.

– Pop would have to find me in the parking lot, snatch me, get me into his car, hide me beneath blankets on the floorboard and drive to a friend's house in Tampa, where we'd all switch cars, and drive to the Orlando airport.

– He'd have to get through security clearance in Orlando and get us on a plane.

– Then he'd have to hope police weren't awaiting the plane's arrival in Atlanta and get us through, then out of the Atlanta airport and to our midtown Atlanta home.

The information was accurate. He succeeded, and it helped that he'd had the forethought to grab Charlotte's keys from the ignition and throw them under the car, preventing her from giving immediate chase.

He also succeeded in hiding me in one car, and then another, and getting me through two major city airports and eventually back to the home I was taken from three days earlier.

Indeed, God was intervening.

Meanwhile, the private investigator Dad had hired urged him to get out of Tampa for a while and let him do his work. Dad isn't so sure that's a good idea.

"You'll get arrested," he told Dad, "and that won't do any of us any good."

"Maybe it would do some good," Dad told him. "Let's find where they are keeping her, make a scene, do whatever we have to do. I'll get arrested and you drive off with Cindy."

Dad is exasperated and not at all patient. But who could blame him? He wants to do something, anything. Retreating out of Tampa equals not doing anything.

"Go to Orlando, Mr. Sanders. Drive back and forth and use the name William Arthur. We'll get eyes on Cindy and figure this thing out. But, not today. You gotta get outta here."

No arrest warrant was issued for my dad, at least as far as he knows.

Nana and Pop are a different story.

When they get back to Atlanta with me, an arrest warrant on kidnapping charges is awaiting them. Fulton County Sheriff Leroy Stynchcombe called Pop to break the news. Pop is friends with the sheriff from church and from the Masonic Lodge. The good-old-boy system was about to work for the good guys in this case.

Stynchcombe heard Pop out and asked him and Nana come to his office to sign an Own Recognizance bond.

"I know you Elt, and I know Billy. As long as what you're telling me is the truth, this will go away," he said. "But keep your head down, would ya? I don't want to have to come bail you out of the jail because you did something stupid. I ain't sure we're that good of friends."

****

Charlotte never was charged, but Nana and Pop were. What must the phone call have done to Dad?

"Charlotte has kidnapped the kids."

As a father, it's hard to stay there for more than a few seconds.

So while Nana and Pop were signing an arrest bond at the Fulton County Sheriff's Department, Dad and the private investigator were thinking of ways to get Cindy back.

I wouldn't ask these questions that day, or the next day, or for the next 43 years. But why did the God who turned Elton Sanders into Chuck Norris for a day, and who cleared every obstacle that would have prevented a successful mission, not see to it that Cindy was rescued that day, too?

By 48 years old, I'd only delved into this story a couple of times, both of which were in seeking healing. I learned to invite Jesus into my wounds, to let Him stir up the hurt and ugliness again in order to provide real, permanent healing. But for the better part of 40 years, the most significant event of my childhood was largely a mystery to me.

If my story were a novel, then all I'd knew was the Cliff Notes version that adults had censored, scrubbing and hidden away. And when your story is a mystery to you, you become a mystery to yourself.

I was raised from age six not to think about "Mom," not to worry about her, not talk about her and not let her have any weight in my life. I went through adolescence and into adulthood with a detached ambiguity toward this woman that both prevented me from hating her and protected me from missing her. I didn't talk about her, or what had happened to me. Not with my best friends growing up, not with my dad, and not with God.

I grew up not knowing my biological mother, and not caring that I didn't know her. I grew up not thinking I needed answers. Now though, I do.

God said:

I've been waiting. None of what happened to you and to Cindy was my will. I did allow it, though. It broke my heart to allow it. But I intervened in a thousand ways that you do not know about. There is a lot that won't be revealed on this side of eternity. But I have lots to say about this. And I have lots to say about you, Cindy and your Dad. So thank you for asking me these questions. I've loved you all so much since the beginning of time.

Chapter 3 – Really God?

"Like an open book, you watched me grow from conception to birth; all the stages of my life were spread out before you, the days of my life all prepared before I'd even lived one day." – Psalms 139: 15-16.

"Go ahead and ask God questions about where He was for this. He let me have my way here. You cannot trust His heart toward you." – The Deceiver

When Charlotte got home from church that morning, minus one of her prisoners, the madness machine began cranking in full force.

"Mary Ellen! We've got to get out of here. We've got to go, now. Now!"

Cindy is told to stay in her room, but she can hear the scheming and panic in the voice of Charlotte and Mary Ellen, and what seemed like some other people, too. She knows that I did not come back to the apartment with Charlotte, but she has no idea what that means other than this: Charlotte and Mary Ellen were manic.

"Get your stuff, Cindy. We're leaving. We've got to get out of here for a while," Charlotte said.

Was something good unfolding? Or something else?

No time for her to dwell on that, or the fact that she was sick. Cindy knew Charlotte and this Mary Ellen woman were not to be trifled with.

But someone was on to what was going on.

Was it private investigators? The FBI?

Again, no time to dwell.

For Charlotte's sick plan to be successful, she couldn't risk staying still. So within hours of my rescue, with Cindy too sick for church, her abductors were on the move, with her in tow.

****

By the time my grandparents got me back to their Atlanta home, my home since shortly after Charlotte had walked out on us, it was clear to all the grown-ups that there wasn't going to be an immediate resolution to the volatile events of the past 72 hours.

"Where's Cindy?" I asked. "Why can't we just go get her?"

To this 6-year-old, it didn't seem like it should be that hard. The kidnapping had shaken me badly. But why we couldn't just go to the police and then go get Cindy was perhaps even more disturbing.

"It's complicated, Sport," my dad said. "We've got the best attorneys working for us."

"Is she going to try to get me again?"

"No," Dad said. "You are safe now. She wouldn't try that again."

"How do you know?"

He didn't know. Truth is, he was scared to death of what Charlotte, her people and her access to money might be able to pull off.

Over the next 18 months or so, my dad would be on the hunt for Cindy, using private investigators, attorneys, cigarettes and Rolaids. His bleeding ulcer got bad enough to make him vomit blood occasionally. At least, I think it was only occasionally.

In 1971, long before the Internet and cell phones, tracking someone was quite different than today. But the specifics of what happened with the investigation and attorneys were a complete mystery to me for 40 years. It was a mystery when I wrote the first chapter of this book. I would investigate my life the best I could, I determined. And then I would tell what I found.

I knew this much though. I was a shattered little boy, clueless about what was going on around me, but wounded and seared by fear.

"Are we close to getting Cindy back?" I asked my dad often.

"We're getting closer," he would say. Every time, it was the same.

"Good. And I'm going to be OK?"

"You are going to be fine, Sport. Nothing's going to happen to you. I won't let it."

My dad's number one goal in these daily conversations had nothing to do with the truth and everything to do with perception.

He wanted to protect his son as much as possible from further emotional angst. That meant lying sometimes. But it always meant overstating his certainty that I was safe and that everything was going to be OK for all of us.

Truth is, he had no idea if I was safe and no idea how things would play out for Cindy. His commitment and passion and sacrifice were never the issue. His ability to use those traits to provide results was very much in question.

In Tampa, the nightmare unfolded little by little.

Cindy was often left alone, all night, on several occasions. She was scared when she was alone at night, but part of her felt safer knowing she was alone in the apartment. Whatever scary people were on the outside probably were less intimidating than the ones on the inside.

Charlotte would lose her temper easily and often without warning. Many a night, after a couple of vodkas, Charlotte would remind Cindy that she was in charge and that she was none too happy with what Cindy was making of her life.

She was spanked, pinched, slapped in the face and had her arms pierced by the fingernails of a crazy woman fully intent on inflicting physical pain. But nothing she did, or maybe could do, would match the emotional and psychological damage already done.

"You aren't very pretty," Charlotte would say. "Look at those buck teeth. You didn't get those teeth from me."

"I know," Cindy would say. "Can I go into my room now?"

"Yeah, go, go. Stay in your room tonight, OK? Mommy's going to have some friends come over and they won't want to see a buck-toothed, chubby little girl."

"Yes ma'am. I'll stay in my room."

As the night would wear on, Cindy would hear noises coming out of Charlotte's room at night, along with the unmistakable – even to a 9-year-old – sounds of sexual acts between Charlotte and Mary Ellen and others.

On a good night, Cindy would only have to hear the sex between Charlotte and Mary Ellen. On a bad night, it was an all-out orgy with people coming and going and the relentless sounds of moaning, cursing and partying.

As a child, Cindy didn't know what to call it. But she knew it wasn't right.

"I was sick to my stomach," Cindy said. "And I'd put pillows over my head and try to go to sleep."

Before Charlotte had abandoned us, Mary Ellen had become a bit of regular at our house. To be more accurate, she had gone from being a visitor of Charlotte's to an ever-present squatter, and usually drunk or high, in a matter of months.

When my dad finally told Charlotte that Mary Ellen had to go, no ifs, ands or buts, she did. And Charlotte left with her.

For decades, I didn't know whether she was Charlotte's lover, a co-dependent druggie, or just a criminal's whacked-out sidekick.

So that might not be where the unraveling of this weird little family began, but it was as close to a starting line as I've ever known. And now she was freaking out Cindy.

Once, while Cindy was left home alone in Tampa, she wrote a letter, addressed it the best she could – we'd both been drilled on our address – and took it to the apartment complex's metal row of mailboxes. She didn't have a key to a mailbox, so she taped it on the front of the boxes with a note: "Please, Mr. Mailman, get this letter to my dad."

The note went something like this:

"I am with Mommy, and I'm not safe here. I'm here alone a lot and that scares me. But maybe you could come get me when she is not here. I want to come home, Daddy."

As far as she knows, the mailman didn't do anything with the letter. There was no stamp on it, and again, no one knew to investigate subtle hints that a child might be in danger. Or perhaps Charlotte or Mary Ellen saw it and took it down. Even if by some miracle of God the letter got to my Dad, odds are it wouldn't have helped.

Still, hearing this story for the first time a few months ago broke my heart. In all the years that she and I have discussed these events, I'd never heard this story. Come to think of it, I'd not heard about the sex parties that went on under her nose. All she had told me, on the occasions we talked specifically about her time there as opposed to Dad's silence, was that Charlotte would insult her a lot and would stay out at night from time to time.

Maybe Cindy had learned the code of silence without even knowing it.

I don't think I ever had survivor's guilt for making it out after three days while she was there 18 months. I think had I heard all her stories, I would have. And I'm not sure I could have bore that on top of everything else.

While Cindy's memories aren't vivid on all the details, she knows they moved several times and that there were various bit players in Charlotte's band of gypsies.

But Cindy had one friend there that she hung out with, a lot – particularly at night and particularly when she was home alone. His name was Jesus.

Cindy had been taught growing up by our dad, Nana and Pop and the preacher at Morningside Baptist Church that Jesus was real, and that she could talk to him like he was her best friend.

Cindy had child-like faith in Jesus, and Jesus loved her like none other. So, on many nights, she would lie in bed and talk to Jesus as if he was sitting in the bed beside her. She was literal in how she believed Jesus was her best friend.

One afternoon, while sitting on the floor of an apartment, she heard Charlotte on the phone with someone, angry and cussing a mile a minute. It frightened Cindy to see that kind of rage.

So she leaned against her bed and said, "Jesus, I know mom is saying bad words and I don't like it. It makes me not want to go to sleep. I know that you are here and will watch over me tonight."

"I'm scared, God," Cindy said. "I'm scared. Talk to me, God. Let me know you are here."

That was her prayer. And she kept saying it over and over. She needed that distraction if nothing else. But she believed it was more than that, even then.

I didn't know this story either.

At times, her prayers were desperate, from a place of fear. But at times, they were flat out mundane, where she'd talk about her day, or about her favorite singer, Donny Osmond.

While Cindy was saying those prayers, in Atlanta, I went to bed scared every night. I'd lie on my side and slowly and rhythmically roll my head from one side to the next while singing Jesus Loves Me, hoping the combination would exhaust me into sleep. When I got tired of singing to myself, I would hum a wordless chant while rolling my head.

It was both comforting and a little disorienting, sort of like taking two Ativans are for me today. This weird nightly ritual, a self-created home remedy for the anxieties of nighttime was the closest I could come to self-medicating as a child and adolescent.

I am embarrassed to say how long that ritual lasted. The real me gets it, that the shame, if there is any to be had, is on the old world that didn't understand childhood issues and psychology and didn't get me help to cope with the anxieties before I took to my own panacea.

Regardless, by the time I stopped rocking myself to sleep, I could do some advanced math, speak enough Spanish to pass a class ... And I was pushing six feet tall.

Yeah, I have plenty of questions I'd like answers to. But I do not have to ask if Jesus was in that room with Cindy all those nights, or if He was lying in bed with me while I rolled around my bed and sang of his love for me.

He was.

He was there for all of it – even the worst of it.

So my question is not so much, "Where were you, God?" because I know He was with us. And I don't really want to ask why He let it happen, because I'm not sure any answer would work for me on this side of eternity.

But I am curious. What were you doing the day we were kidnapped, God?

I know we were supposedly going to Lenox Mall to shop. It was my first time seeing Charlotte since she walked out on our family. But what about you, God? Why weren't you doing more?

What about on the car ride to the airport when I was so scared and sad? I was six years old!

And what kind of sick, master rescue plan leaves Cindy trapped in Tampa, away from her home, for 18 months?

That I can sit here today and think about all of the abductions since mine, the ones that were so much more horrific, where kids were chained in basements for years and raped or tortured, doesn't lessen my abduction, God. You know that, right?

I don't think I was chained to anything, or sexually assaulted. But I don't know.

I ask these questions now not fully knowing any of the answers. But I'm getting closer on a lot of them.

But I have to be able to fill in the blanks to tell this story and the effect it has had on me, and thus on my wife and daughters. It affected my parenting and the job I've done as a husband.

My grandmother would have told me the story as best as she knew it, had I asked. She's been dead since 1996, though.

My grandfather died in 2011 at the age of 100. I'm not sure what he would have told me had I asked. He was a strong man, a good man, and obviously a hero in my story. But I don't think his era saw the need in talking things through. So that sleeping dog lied.

Not talking about it with Pop meant I never thanked him, specifically, for what he did for me. But he knew I loved him.

The only person on earth who knows most of this is my dad. Of course, he wasn't there in Tampa that weekend, so he doesn't know about that. But he knows an awful lot, more than he's ever told Cindy or me.

It would be easy for me to ask him – easy for me, painful for him.

For years, I didn't know the extent of damage I'd do in bringing this up with him. I know he's an outgoing, gregarious man who never met a stranger. But he's as fragile as I am, maybe more so. He's been deeply wounded by fighting a battle that, as a father now, I couldn't imagine having to fight. In fact, I can better understand now why my dad wanted to protect my fragile psyche. Hiding scary truths from my kids has been my most noble mistake.

But in avoiding and evading, Dad was inadvertently laying the groundwork for a lifetime of keeping things inside, covered up, and not discussed. It was as if it wasn't talked about, it didn't happen. Thus, for the rest of my life, up until now anyway, the life-changing events of 1971 through 1973 were not discussed.

I imagine some of it was guilt and shame on his part – guilt and shame for what, I don't know. For doing the best he could and that not being good enough? Maybe. That was a sentiment I'd become familiar with, as well.

I'd sooner die than go through what he went through. I imagine he'd have sooner died, too. He had a bleeding ulcer in his stomach by the time he was 32. He has had a tremor as long as I can remember. He is in remission from bladder cancer. And he has buried that part of our lives, deeply and definitively. He's 74 years old now. I don't know if he can handle me asking the questions I need to ask.

What do you have to say about that one, God?

God said: *"I'm about to amaze you."*

He was right.

God said:

I was there. I was in the car the day you and Cindy were driven away from your home and into abduction. I knew exactly how it was going to play out. I knew the tears that you'd cry and the years of hurt and confusion that would all stem from this day.

That has to be on the table to begin with. I could've changed it. I could've prevented it. I could have caused Charlotte to have a flat tire before she ever got to Nana and Pop's house. And I could have placed an unquenchable thirst in their hearts to take you two to Six Flags that day after the flat tire. I could've made it the best day of your young lives.

I was capable of doing all of that and so much more. But I didn't.

I know you won't ever fully understand why I allowed this to happen, not until I can explain it to you with all of eternity as a backdrop. And I'll do that. I promise. And it will bring no tears, no confusion and no angst.

Don't miss this, though, Bill: I loved you and Cindy, and still do, with a love that is extravagant, never-ending and isn't dependent upon anything you do, or even upon whether you love me back. What was I doing that day in Atlanta? What was I doing for the next 18 excruciating months? I was holding you close to me. I cried with you in the car ride to the airport and stroked your hair. I cleared at least a dozen obstacles for Pop to make his heroic rescue and get you back to Atlanta. I kept Cindy company on many a lonely, scary night.

I kept thinking of the new and marvelous ways I would bring good out of this wretchedly bad event. I began lining up people that I wanted you to meet, and to minister to, 10, 20, 30 years down the road. I thought about Jane that day in 1971. I thought a lot about Rachel and Laura and the kind of daddy they were going to need.

Even though I knew how this was going to end, it was still crushing my heart to let it happen. I knew that what others had meant for bad, I meant for good. We were together that day Bill, and every day before and since. I wanted to remind you of that.

Chapter 4 – Courtrooms

"I have summoned you by name; you are mine."
– Isaiah 43:1

*"You were a weak kid and no matter what
happened, you'll become a weak man."*
– The Deceiver

After my kidnapping and rescuing, one would imagine that the single most dramatic day was behind me. One would be wrong.

In early 1973, with Cindy as one prisoner, Charlotte filed a lawsuit seeking return of the second half of her spoils – me.

She claimed my dad had unlawful custody of me, and she was demanding legal authority to reclaim what was briefly hers, presumably to wield more power over my dad and gain more financial control.

In the lawsuit, Charlotte stated she had "demanded the return of her child from the defendants, but they have refused to return her child to her." She claimed "that on or around August 15 of that year, that A.E. and Era Sanders (Pop and Nana) grabbed me from her and forcibly removed me to Fulton County without her consent."

That part was true.

The suit asked a Fulton County judge to "command and require the defendants to produce the person of her child, William Arthur Sanders Jr., before this court by law, and that her former husband, William Arthur Sanders, be required to pay support payments for the future support of this child."

Fulton County Superior Court Judge Elmo Holt agreed, at least to the first part.

On January 18, 1973, my dad and grandparents were "hereby commanded to produce the body of William Arthur Sanders Jr., alleged to be illegally detained by you, together with the cause of detention, before Superior Court Judge Osgood Williams on Feb. 2, 1973, at 9:30 a.m."

The next part of the sentence had to be the scariest for my dad.

"... then and there to be disposed of as the law directs."

Then and there, my body was to be produced and my fate determined.

Court filings that led up to Judge Holt's ruling were convoluted and state-centric. Dad had filed for divorce in North Carolina and in Georgia, based on abandonment. Charlotte had filed in Florida, basing her case on working the intricacies of the system. In her divorce suit, Charlotte claimed "the award of the custody of the two minor children to her former husband (by the Georgia judge) is not valid because petitioner was never served in person."

That was true, too, but deceptively true, Charlotte-true. Dad's divorce papers had been legally published in the newspaper of record, which was common in the '70s. But serving someone who is constantly on the move is tricky, and Cindy remembers Charlotte on more than one occasion talking about how they had to stay on the move so she wouldn't get served with papers.

Eventually, a Florida judge granted Charlotte custody of Cindy and me; a Georgia judge had granted custody to my dad.

But now that a Georgia judge was in agreement that Dad had to show up in court, with me in tow, and essentially prove that he was the more-fit parent– not an easy task for a father now, a near-impossible one in 1973 – all the previous filings and rulings essentially were moot.

I can't imagine what kind of hell this must've been for Dad. After all he'd been through, after the miraculous events that got me back to him and Nana and Pop's, all of that was up for grabs again on February 2, 1973.

I've asked him about that. His answers are short but intense, sort of like talking to a war vet who's seen things he'd rather not talk about.

"Yeah, I was scared," Dad said. "It was awful. That morning, going to court…No words for it. The worst of the worst."

Asking him about that morning and hearing his sparse response was perhaps the most gut-wrenching conversation we had, for both of us. I couldn't help but put myself in his shoes and wonder if I'd had the fortitude to keep my wits about me.

Imagining how I'd deal with it somehow begins to seem selfish though. So I take myself out of the equation and think only about Dad. He was convinced that he wasn't only at risk of losing me, he was at risk of losing me to a dangerous, reckless women and an unhealthy environment, one in which he didn't think I could survive.

So this was far from a he-said/she-said showdown. It was good vs. evil, sanity vs. craziness.

"We don't have any choice," Dad's attorney, Willard Shelfer told him. "You've got to be there on February 2. And you've got to take Bill Jr."

"What's it mean, Willard? Then and there to be disposed of? That doesn't mean..."

"Let's not get ahead of ourselves," Shelfer said.

"You're the one who told me how hard it was for the fathers to get custody of the kids and now a judge is telling me to bring Bill to court? And I might not bring him home with me that day? Don't get ahead of myself?"

"She's made it clear that this is about money," Shelfer said. "The judge will see that. Listen Bill. If you'd asked me a year ago whether you could go into a courtroom against the boy's mama and come out a winner, I'd have told you, 'Hell, no! It won't happen. But I think we've got a real chance here, Bill."

"I don't know," my dad said. "I don't have this kind of money, and neither do Mom and Dad, but we can pay her. That's what she wants anyway. I'll write her a check for $5,000, no make it, $10,000. I just want my kids."

"I don't know, Bill, but it might work. Let me get on it."

Within days he had a document signed by Charlotte and her attorney.

The cringe-worthy offer, and the even more cringe-worthy acceptance of an offer, might have sounded good to Shelfer Jr., since he knew the depths of Dad's desperation. And since it was what Charlotte was going after all along, somehow it sounded good to Hambrick.

But Shelfer's dad, Willard Shelfer Sr., was the wiser and steadier hand of the legal team. Junior was doing most of the grunt work, but senior had to sign off on big decisions. Trying to buy a child –though it was nobler than it sounds – qualified as a big decision. It just didn't make sense long term.

"No," the elder Shelfer said. "Not only no, but hell, no. Bill, I get your desperation. But Willard, you know better. No judge in the state is gonna sign off on that. It's buying a kid, for God's sake. If I take that to Judge Osgood, he'll hold it against us, and I wouldn't blame him.

Then to my dad: "I think we've got better than a puncher's chance here, Bill. But we gotta keep it together, show up early, be respectful, and we'll put Charlotte on the stand and ask her about Mary Ellen."

"She'll lie," Dad said.

"Let's hope so," Shelfer Sr. said. "If she does, you'll walk out with your boy."

"I'm scared to death, ya know?" Dad said.

"I know you are. I would be, too. But liars lie. Let's count on that."

******

Dana Burns, a Presbyterian elder, a Navy veteran and a man's man, wanted to believe his daughter. He'd wanted to believe her for years. And for years, she'd let him down and prove herself untrustworthy.

To me, Mr. Burns was a towering physical specimen, 6-foot 3-inches or so, with jet-black hair and an olive complexion. I don't remember him well, but my vague recollections are that he seemed much closer to a no-nonsense authoritarian than a cuddly granddad. His study, or den, was in rich mahogany wood and dark burgundy leathers. I remember the smell of a pipe. I do not remember ever running and jumping into his arms, or him ever seeing me as someone to get on the floor and play with.

Before the kidnapping, Dad said he took Cindy and me to see the Burns every Sunday after church. After the kidnapping, he appealed to Mr. Burns' sensibilities.

"I asked him why he allowed this to happen and he said it looked bad on his family name for Charlotte not to have the kids," Dad told me.

So there was that.

A compilation of interviews leads me to believe this Mr. Burns entered the courtroom that morning wanting to keep some dignity for the family name, but was also holding onto a shred of belief that his daughter was not the out-of-control, heavy-drinking, free-living young woman who had such disregard for the collateral damage that was his grandchildren.

But grasping at shreds of belief rarely ends well.

Mr. Burns would later tell his wife and Claire, his version of the morning this way:

"Baby, I need to know everything there is to know," he told Charlotte before the hearing.

"You do, Daddy," she said. "I promise, Daddy. You know everything."

"Nothing's going to surprise me or embarrass me today, is it?"

"No, Daddy. Don't be silly."

Mr. Burns had his reasons for being a little leery of Charlotte's innocent act.

He had gotten his introduction to Mary Ellen's influence on Charlotte one day when they stopped in Athens, Ga., to pick up a defiant Charlotte from college and take her with them to Asheville, N.C., where her grandparents were celebrating their 50th wedding anniversary.

Charlotte had told her dad she didn't want to go. First she said she had too much schoolwork. Then she said she was sick. Mr. Burns got madder with every excuse and showed up unannounced, willing to drag her to the car by her scalp, if necessary.

What he found was Charlotte in Mary Ellen's dorm room, in her bed and under the covers. Mary Ellen was making excuses, but Mr. Burns knew what was going on, and it didn't jibe with his Presbyterian and military values – particularly not in the early '60s.

Mary Ellen's background was similar to Charlotte's in at least one manner. Social status was a big deal in her family. A member of the Tampa Yacht and Country Club and the Tampa Junior Women's Club, Mary Ellen had been given every chance to succeed in life. Frank and Lucille Cochran adopted Mary Ellen as a baby in 1937. Somewhere between then and 1961 though, Mary Ellen took a serious liking to alcohol and drugs. Who knows what was in her genetic background, but she was not on the successful, philanthropic path that Frank and Lucille had laid.

And while this was the first proof of Charlotte's promiscuity, from what I have since been told, it was only the latest in a decade of mistrust and misbehavior

So now, with Mary Ellen back in the picture, Mr. Burns was torn. He had money and was using it to fund Charlotte's legal fees. He wanted so much to believe what she was saying to him – like almost any father would. But the odds were stacked that she was hiding something. Somewhere deep down, Mr. Burns knew it.

Shortly after 9:30 a.m. on February 2, 1973, William Shelfer Sr. called Charlotte to the witness stand.

"Ms. Burns, I only have a couple of questions for you. It won't take but a minute.

"OK."

"Do you know a woman named Mary Ellen Cochran?"

"I do."

"How do you know her?"

"We went to college together."

"Is that it?" Shelfer asked.

"Yes."

"Is there nothing else about your relationship with Mary Ellen that the court should know?"

"She's a friend. I've visited her and she's visited me when Bill and I were married. She's had some hard times and she needed a friend. That's it."

"Thank you, Miss. Burns, nothing further. Your honor, we'd like to introduce six letters that Charlotte and Mary Ellen wrote to each other over the past year."

"Objection, your honor," Charlotte's attorney, Claude Hambrick, said.

"I'm going to look at the letters and decide whether to consider it, Claude."

I had never heard of "the letters" before my in-depth interview with Dad in January 2014. Even after that, the contents of the letters remained a mystery to me. But these letters mattered. A lot.

According to Dad, Charlotte had given the letters, one at a time, for Dad to mail for her, from his office over a period of a couple of months. Instead of mailing them, he kept the unopened letters in a manila envelope, as potential evidence in what was looking like an inevitable divorce, and custody proceeding. Dad says he never opened the letters, and thus never read them, because he assumed that keeping them sealed would cause them to be seen as more credible and authentic should he ever need them.

I'm pretty sure he'd put two and two together by then and had reason to think the letters might call into question Charlotte's character.

It didn't take Judge Williams more than a minute or two on the bench looking at the letters. He called Mr. Burns, Hambrick, Shelfer and Charlotte into his chambers. Dad wasn't invited.

Within about a half hour, they came out.

"You've got custody of your son Bill," Shelfer Sr. said. "It's done. We've got it in writing. Claude signed it, I signed it and the judge signed it."

My dad began to cry.

I was in the courthouse with Nana and Pop, but not in the courtroom. I had no idea what was going on other than I might have to take the stand and state my preference on who I wanted to live with.

"Bill, that's not all," Shelfer said. "Judge Williams is filing a notice with Gwinnett County Judge Michael Reed, asking that he have Cindy arrested tonight and brought before the my court on Monday morning for a similar hearing. And don't worry; I shouldn't have even used the word arrested. That's their term. Obviously, she's not going to be charged with a crime, but they are taking custody of her."

Our side of the family left the courthouse relieved, and for the first time in 18 months, hope was overcoming fear.

Mr. Burns left the courthouse a shell of the man he was hours earlier. The shreds of hope that Charlotte wasn't who he suspected she had become evaporated.

He died a little that day, and every day for the next 35 years. I'm told he never loved Charlotte another day of her life. He helped her out from time to time, and was cordial mostly, but whether it was love that he had lost, or trust, or respect – that is semantics. The relationship was irrevocably damaged.

The letters that pushed Judge Williams so firmly to my dad's side were sealed and maybe no longer exist. But apparently they were bad – way worse than love letters between two women in the early '70s. Then again, those letters might have saved my life.

****

This night, Friday, February 2, 1973 was already looking like a pretty decent night for Cindy. For one thing, The Partridge Family was on. And while David Cassidy wasn't Donny Osmond, he wasn't a bad consolation prize either.

The apartment was quiet, too. Whatever Charlotte was up to on this night, it didn't involve Cindy, or lots of people, and at least so far, no yelling. Cindy had no idea that so much was going on behind the scenes, on various fronts. The wheels of justice were in motion. But so were the conniving wheels of deceit.

In her pajamas, on the twin bed and watching the small black-and-white TV, right in the middle of The Partridge Family, two Gwinnett County Sheriff's Department deputies appeared on the patio, just outside Cindy's bedroom.

They knocked on the sliding glass door. Cindy got up and opened the door. By now, it took a lot to shock Cindy. Two deputies knocking on the sliding glass door on a Friday night didn't rank in the top 100.

"Are you Cindy Sanders?" one of the officers asked.

"Yes, sir."

"You need to come with me. Grab your robe and come with me, now."

Cindy obliged, unsure of whether this was something good or bad. Had she participated in something? Was she in trouble for something Charlotte had done? But with uncertainty comes hope. The devil she didn't know – the darkness of night and two armed deputies –seemed more appealing than the devil she knew.

"Is your dad Bill Sanders?"

"Yes, sir."

"He waiting up at the top of the hill for you."

But Dad had strict orders from the cops and courts. He could speak to Cindy, tell her things were going to be OK, but he was not taking her home. Deputies were taking Cindy to a third-party safe house until the Gwinnett County judge and the Fulton County judge worked things out and brought Cindy before Fulton County Superior Court Judge Williams.

The court hearing scheduled for Monday never happened. On Sunday afternoon, Shelfer Sr. called my dad.

"Go pick up your daughter, Bill. It's over. They've signed custody over to you."

Two things that probably will go unanswered for eternity – exactly what happened in Judge Williams' chambers that Friday morning and what caused Charlotte to give up the fight and hand Cindy over to my dad that Sunday?

"Mr. Burns was a smart man, and I really think not a bad guy except for how much he valued his status above all else," Dad said. "I think he and Mr. Hambrick convinced Charlotte that she was about to be in a bucket of worms. I never talked to Charlotte that Friday, that weekend, or ever since."

We never saw the Burns again either.

When Mr. Burns died in August 2001, the obituary stated his survivors included two children and two grandchildren. One of Charlotte's sisters, Jan, never married and died at age 27. For more than half of her life, she had battled health issues, losing more of them than she won. Her other sister, Claire has twin sons. Those were the grandchildren listed in the obit.

God said:

First, about the obit. It doesn't matter whether Mr. Burns recognized you. You were, are and always will be mine. I will never deny you or fail to brag about you with gusto. I guided Sheriff Stynchcombe toward kindness, guided your grandparents toward courage and kept your dad alive. I'm so proud of your dad, by the way. I'm proud of you for knowing him in this new way, and proud of him for letting himself be known like this. I chose him to be your father because I knew you were going to need one of the best. He was, and remains, flawed. So were all of the heroes of the Bible. You don't realize, even now, what he is sacrificing by opening up this way to you. Enjoy this new season of relationship. That's what it's there for.

Chapter 5 – Reunited

"Anyone who loves their brother and sister lives in the light, and there is nothing in them to make them stumble." – I John 2:10

"You learned two lessons from your mommy and your nana. They were right. Don't forget it." – The Deceiver

Before we got Cindy back, I slept most nights either in a daybed in the dining room or with Nana or Pop – never both, because, well, that would just be weird.

And yes, a daybed in the dining room is as odd as it sounds. But it didn't seem out of the ordinary to a little boy who knew no ordinary. Plus, it was closer to Nana and Pop's room. So night when I was feeling brave, I'd sleep there.

When Dad was home, I'd often sleep upstairs in an efficiency-type bedroom with my dad. That was a treat because there was a television in his room and because I could give my anxieties the night off.

I was grasping to cling to anything that seemed routine and safe to me. One of those things was Friday night Bridge game at Nana and Pop's.

Mr. and Mrs. Vaughn were two of the fattest people I'd ever seen in my young life. Mr. Vaughn, I'm pretty sure had false teeth too. But they were jolly, they were familiar and they played a mean game of Bridge in my grandparent's living room. I'd lie in my grandparents' bed and watch the Bob Newhart Show while life, laughter and fellowship was going on in the room next to me. I liked that feeling. I liked that I knew that Friday it was going to happen, just like the week before.

I also like it because the more friendlies in the house, the less likely someone would break into the house, overpower Nana and Pop and take me.

This was about the time I first made my own assessment of who I was and what I was about. I was not ready to be the man of the house, or even the man of the room. I got a sick feeling in my gut whenever my dad would remind me to be the man of the house while he was gone. I wasn't up to that task. No kid my age is. I was at my best in the daylight and with someone I trusted within shouting distance.

But other than those peculiarities, my needs really weren't that excessive.

I loved baseball cards, more than almost anyone I knew. I didn't collect them to keep in mint condition for future investments (that was the next generation of collectors) or to put in the spokes of my bicycle (that must have been the previous generation, if it ever really existed outside of the movies or TV shows). I collected them because I liked to play with them. I like to look at the faces of players and study their statistics. But mostly I liked to play general manager and draft teams. For those who play fantasy football, it was my own little fantasy league, and for once, I was about 25 years ahead of my time.

Even without baseball cards, I was pretty adept at entertaining myself. Oftentimes, I would get on the floor at Nana and Pop's house and play with pencils, preferably new ones that had not been sharpened, and preferably something other than the standard yellow pencil. I would pretend the pencils were professional wrestlers.

Back up for a second. As I kid, I really liked watching professional wrestling on TV. We would go to the old Atlanta Arena a couple of times with Pop to see the likes of Professor Tara Tanaka, Cowboy Bob Watts and Abdullah the Butcher. I was afraid in the arena. I kind of, sort of, knew professional wrestling was fake, even as a little boy. But I wasn't sure. And if I was wrong about that, I wasn't at all sure Pop could protect me if things got out of hand and the Butcher or Ox Baker decided to take out some of their anger on a skinny 7-year-old with a ridiculously high hair line and at least two cowlicks.

I always wanted to leave before the main event, not because I was sleepy or bored, but because getting out of their before the mayhem climaxed just seemed to make sense to me.

I don't know if many little boys 40 years ago, or today, really live the carefree, secure life that we hope kids experience before the world gets cruel. It seemed like everyone but my dad and I were pretty carefree.

That might be what attracted me to wrestling as a child. I wanted to be someone who was confident, tough and knew that I was able to take care of myself. That is not how I saw myself for years to come.

About this same time in life, I also became acutely aware that Dr. John Dixon, of Oakdale, was conniving and could not be trusted. No eight- or nine-year old boy should have spent so much time with the crew from the fictional town of Oakdale. But Nana loved her "stories," and from 1:30 to 2:30 was the most important one – As The World Turns.Pop watched them, too, but he pretended it was only to placate Nana. That pretense worked on me then. But I know better now.

****

I prayed for Cindy's safe return every night, as did my dad and grandparents. But when that day finally arrived, it was nothing short of, well, weird. I was a seven-year-old who had not seen his sister in a well over a year. She wasn't a stranger to me, but at first, she was more like an adopted sister, or some kind of a welcomed addition to my family. But just that, an addition.

And I wasn't sure she was sticking around.

It wasn't comfortable around the house, for more than a little while, Everyone was walking on eggshells, not sure how to interact with each other and maybe not even sure how to feel. What is the right way to act when such a long, messed-up situation comes to an end? Happy? Thankful? I felt those things, as did everyone. But it was weird, largely, I think, because we were in the early stages of pretending this never happened,

I was too young to read a lot into anything, so I could just go on what I saw. Pop acted fine. Pop. He was happy Cindy was home, but not all gushy about it. In fact, he could still display some of the gruffness of an old farm hand and government man, which he was. In other words, Pop was being Pop, which provided some normalcy and comfort.

Nana on the other hand was stiff and cool toward Cindy, which I know was hard for Cindy. It was hard for me to watch and process. For the past 18 months or so, Nana had had a son to raise again – even if I was her grandson, and even if Dad was still in charge when he was around. It filled an emotional hole for her that I didn't recognize at all as an 8-year-old. By time I was a teenager I could see this but not put a name to it. By the time Cindy and I were adults, it had become a widely accepted fact among my family.

Cindy, on some level, was throwing all of that out of balance.

Nana was jealous, insecure and manipulative – traits of an un- diagnosed emotional disorder we now know she had. I was the primary focus of her attention because of how it fed her needs. I was the one who needed her the most, she determined. I was the one who needed to be protected the most. No one was going to take that from her. Not Dad, not Pop and certainly not the return of Cindy, who by the way, looked a fair amount like Charlotte.

Both of them would spank Cindy – not violently and not with anything other than a switch, a hand, or once a towel that turned into a makeshift whip. I might have gotten spanked, too. I don't think so, though.

Pop's preferred method of corporal punishment being a thump to the head, which I did get on more than one occasion, and usually because I was squirming or chatting during church. I've never been able to thump someone on the head and have it hurt them worse than it'd hurt my finger. Not that I ever remember wanting to, but still. I guess it might have come in handy a time or two.

Truth be told, though, Nana loved me more than she loved Cindy. And it showed. And that's not a good place for either kid. Inadvertently, she was the first to give me a new name. I was The One Who Needed To Be Taken Care Of. That doesn't exactly roll off the tongue. And no one ever hollered to me, "Hey, The One Who Needed To Be Taken Care Of, it's dinner time."

But she babied me. By subtly mothering-by-smothering me, she was reinforcing what I was taught when I was five years old, and that was that I didn't have what it takes.

Charlotte taught me that I didn't have what it took to make a mom stay and Nana was teaching me that I didn't have what it took to have an age-appropriate level of independence and autonomy.

Even though I didn't recognize it at the time, I was longing for a new name, one that only God could give.

But regardless of the Nana dynamics, from the first day that Cindy was back, I knew we shared a bond that would keep us close to one another for the rest of our lives. And I loved her very much.

Cindy and I lived in a room that Nana and Pop added on to the side of the dining room. To help you get the picture fully, you could stand at the daybed in the dining room and look straight ahead, past the dining room table to our bedroom, which was four steps above the dining room, with a sliding glass door and a sheer curtain for privacy. The house was stone. The add-on bedroom was plywood and siding and essentially was standing on four stilts. It looked more like a tree house that had been super glued to the backside of the house. But oddly, it seemed to fit this house, probably because the décor of the house could best be described as weird.

Despite it being on stilts and almost certainly not being up to any building code, Cindy and I felt about as safe as we ever had. She had posters of Donny Osmond on the walls and played Alice Cooper's *Welcome to My Nightmare* on the record player. Strange bedfellows in any other house, but it seemed about right in ours.

For both Cindy and me, the best thing about the reuniting was that I had a roommate and no longer slept in the dining room, and she had a roommate and no longer had to hear crazy noises from down the hall.

As you'd imagine, Cindy had trouble sleeping, as did I. But sleepless nights, together, weren't nearly as scary as they were alone. We'd try to combat those scary nights by singing and praying together. During the spring and summer, we'd go to sleep listening to the Braves on a transistor radio. At least a handful of times, we would both find ourselves awake at the same time in the middle of the night. That seemed so cool that we'd tell each other that we'd talk sometime in the middle of the night and we pretended that it would happen every night.

Cindy became so accustomed to my head rolling and chanting hum, that she insists to this day it's why she likes to have white noise while she sleeps. She knew as a child that it was my way of shutting out the world and escaping into exhaustion. But somehow that memory brings her comfort instead of taking her to a bad place. I guess it speaks to the power of togetherness.

God said:

Not everyone has a relationship with his sister like you do. It's just a small piece of the good that has come from the wretched. Without that bond, you don't know what would have become of Cindy through the years. I do know. You don't know how her children would have been impacted because their mother wasn't the exact Cindy she is because of this relationship. I do. Or what about the friends of her children that were impacted by their faithfulness? You don't even know their names. I know every hair on their head. The ripple effect of everything that I have allowed in your life, and in Cindy's life, one day you'll see. And you're going to be amazed. I can't wait to show you. Oh, and speaking of amazed, tell your friends to Google Alice Cooper and Christian. Pretty cool, huh?

Chapter 6 – Wounds

"He heals the brokenhearted and binds up their wounds." – Psalms 147:3

"Wounds? What wounds? Quit being a sissy."
– The Deceiver

Time heals all wounds."

That's what they say. In what fantasy world does time heal everything?

As you may have learned by now, time does not heal all wounds. It might dull the harsh sting, or replace one wound with another, making us all but forget the initial wound that never quite healed.

But only God heals wounds. And if we're honest, He doesn't always heal all our wounds, at least not on earth. And He often doesn't heal my hurts until I've invited Him into the wound, and am willing to have the scab ripped back off, feel the deep and acute burn again, that it is healed once and for all.

Author John Eldredge says, "A wound that goes unacknowledged and unwept is a wound that cannot heal."

For the better part of four decades, my wound went unacknowledged and unwept. Not only was I never taught how to deal with it, like many, I was taught not to acknowledge it. Most men come from long lines of men not dealing with their internal wounds. My dad was taught that. And I imagine Pop was raised that was too. So I don't blame them for modeling this. But I never knew a better way.

The late Christian author and speaker Brennan Manning, a man willing to be stunningly vulnerable about his tortured soul, wrote so simply and beautifully about woundedness:

"In a futile attempt to erase our past, we deprive the community of our healing gift," he wrote in Abba's Heart. "If we conceal our wounds out of fear and shame, our inner darkness can neither be illuminated, nor become a light for others."

My fear of what I might find was my motivation for four decades of hiding. For my dad, I think it was his shame about what I might find, along with his hopes that I'd not be hurt further.

Pastor and author Rick Warren, whose emotionally ill son took his life in 2013, says God never wastes a hurt. Warren says he saw himself one day becoming a spokesman for mental health. He prayed he'd never have to become a spokesman on suicide. Now he's both.

But to suffer in silence and not allow others to find help or encouragement from a horrible circumstance or a screwed up childhood is selfish. It robs others of the chance to define and identify their pain through our words. And it eliminates the chance to then see that God remained faithful, in the seemingly bottomless pit of our despair.

Warren was quick to understand that. I feel a little late to that party, but God assures me I'm right on time. Let me just say, if you're looking for escape from the pain or despair you're in and you aren't finding it, I get it.

If you need control over your circumstances and can't seem to get hold of them, I get that too.

I don't know why God allows the abandonment, the loss of a child, the infidelity of a spouse, or whatever. All I know is that is often what brings us to realize we desperately need rescuing. Is that why He allows what he does? I think He allows way less than we think, but its still way more than we wish.

But it's always for a purpose. And maybe it's even necessary.

My dad traveled a lot for business. Often, he was gone from Sunday night until Friday night. Even though I felt at home at Nana and Pop's house, it broke my heart every time he kissed me goodbye and said, "See you Friday night, Sport."

From the time we had gotten Cindy back through fifth grade, that was my lot in life. Pretty soon though, I learned not to cry when he left. By the time I was 10 or 11, I didn't feel it so much anymore. Is that how time heals wounds, by ensuring even a little boy covers up his heart to keep it from being broken so many times?

I never felt good about him leaving. I never felt the same level of safety or security around the house when he was gone.

My grandparents took fine care of Cindy and me. But how could he not be home every night after all that Cindy and I had been through? Surely there were sales jobs that wouldn't require him to travel every week.

His job moved us from Atlanta to Birmingham, and then less than a year later, from Birmingham to Orlando.

Isn't that kind of close to Tampa? I thought.

The word "Tampa" scared me. For years, I would get chills when "Tampa" came up in conversation.

The Orlando years were awkward, but mostly for the normal domestic weirdness of a house with a 13-year-old girl, a 10-year-old boy, two grandparents and a sometime-home dad.

But time healed nothing.

Here's what I know now that I didn't know then. Abandonment creates a different wound than abduction.

Because I was abandoned, I grew up desperate for love. I'd do anything for people to even like me. I'd seek them out, anticipating that they eventually wouldn't like me, but hoping I could continue to fool them. And this abandonment residue – a film that I'm constantly trying to wash off me – is merely an irritant compared to the thick sludge left all over me from being kidnapped.

Being kidnapped taught me to live afraid. Every kid learns fear in some way, but it became my defining characteristic. Because fear was left to run amok in my life for decades, it has become my ever-present tormentor.

However, it will never be the truest part of me. Throughout the years, the true me was, is and will be a beloved child of the King of Kings, made in His image. I was created to carry light and be a shining reflection of God. But this weighty burden unchecked for 40 years has become my default.

The kid I was in Orlando who was about to move back to the Atlanta area, knew none of this. But the 48-year-old me knows it well. Being abandoned was going to be an annoyance that would surface from time to time and need to be addressed. In the grand scheme of my life, it was going to be the medical equivalent of a heat rash, or a little acne, or maybe a recurring mild case of tonsillitis.

Being stolen away from my home and my dad? That was going to be the equivalent of losing my left lung. I'd live through it, but not without lots of gasping.

I can't put my finger on the moment my innocence was first stripped away. It happens to kids little by little in even the most stable of households. I imagine for me, it was being chipped away from before Charlotte left. Certainly before she stole us.

I'm sure of this though: The loss of innocence we all experience, in our own way, is why we need hope of something better. It's why our hearts quietly ache for Eden. Without the loss of innocence, we'd not need a savior. Or at least we wouldn't recognize it.

And in my life, it's altogether possible I would have never known the true value of staying had I not been abandoned.

Someone who stays with you even in the worst of circumstances expresses the difference between what most people think of as love and the real, unconditional kind. I know that essential distinction like I know my own name. So is that something of what it looks like when He works all things, including the vile ones, together for good?

Maybe time healed nothing. But it provided space for God to work, and the chance for perspective, which in turn allowed me to recognize this truth. I am constantly being molded, and the work He is doing in my life is far from completed. The emotional wounds are no longer enough to cause regular pain. But unlike wounds on the physical body, where scars provide a tough covering, internal wounds can still be reopened from time to time.

God said:

It was hell for your dad. He was a great Stayer, but him being away so much caused you to recognize that when you become a father, and when Rachel needs you to be under the same roof as her every night, you'll choose to do that. You'll see Rachel's irrational insecurity and fears, and they won't seem so irrational. Your dad made huge sacrifices; you know that now. But you'll make some that your dad didn't think about making. You will turn down opportunities to be a beat writer for a college or pro team because the travel it would require. At the time, it won't seem like much of a sacrifice. But it's something you learned from the mistakes of your dad.

And Rachel and Laura? They'll learn a lot from you too. Much of it will be from you making sacrifices and being there. But they're also going to learn from your mistakes and poor choices. Remember for your dad, and for you, love covers a multitude of sins. It also covers a multitude of boneheaded, honest mistakes.

Chapter 7 – Dad

"Sons are a heritage from the LORD, children a reward from him. Like arrows in the hands of a warrior are sons born in one's youth." – Psalms 127: 3-4

"Seriously? Of course, you were, and still are, a disappointment to your dad." – The Deceiver

In the book *Beautiful Boy*, author David Sheff beings with this quote from Thomas Lynch: "It hurts so bad that I cannot save him, protect him, keep him out of harm's way, shield him from pain. What good are fathers if not for these things?"

Replace "him" with "them" and the quote, born out of a deep longing to not only do more, but to *be* more, could've been coined by my dad. Or by me. Or likely, by any true father. Any parent experiences it. For me, it gives voice to my daily lament.

My dad surely asked the question often in the early '70s. And that blows my mind away. How could he wonder of his import and value to us amidst this battle? Sure, I wished he were home more. But this is a man who would show me what staying meant long before I knew staying was ever a choice.

He's also a man who had many opportunities to be disappointed in his son. And he could have if he'd used some more traditional lenses. But he never did.

Fathers, good ones at least, always wish for something more and better for their children than what they had. I'm sure my dad had those hopes. And if you were to ask him, he'd insist there were countless ways I surpassed him, and exceeded any bar he'd subconsciously   set.

But there are some realities that even he can't deny. For starters, he was a much better athlete than me. He was an all-city baseball and football player at Atlanta's Grady High School. He played for Erk Russell, who later became the famed defensive coordinator at the University of Georgia and went on to win a 1-AA national championship at Georgia Southern University.

Dad was a good enough football player to be invited to summer practice at Auburn University in 1958, the year Russell had left Grady to be an assistant at Auburn. He was a good enough baseball player to be scouted by pro teams. Ultimately, a serious knee injury and the inability to hit a curve ball with regularity prevented him from advancing to the next levels.

By comparison, I never made the high school basketball

team (the only high school team I ever tried out for). Not only could I not hit the curve ball, I couldn't hit a fastball – even a lame one. I played one season, in third grade, and got hit more times that I got a hit. For me, baseball seemed best to be watched, not played.

I never tried football except for a year of flag football in fifth grade. I was pretty good at flag football and was pretty good at backyard football, even when we were playing tackle. I wasn't very fast, but was always stronger than most. I was just lacking in nastiness and the desire to play with reckless abandon for my body.

I was pretty good at basketball, just not good enough. And I became pretty good at tennis. Just not great. And eventually, I could lift way more weight at the gym than my dad ever could. But then again, he never really tried.

I'm not bemoaning those truths. I'm just saying that had my dad placed lofty athletic expectations on me, he'd have been disappointed.

My dad is also considered one of the most outgoing and friendly guys that most people know. He'd say he's shy, and actually I believe him. You have to know him like a son or a wife to realize that he is shy. No one else would buy it for a minute because he has a gift at overcoming that shyness that allowed him a good level of success in the sales world and continues to work in his favor at cocktail and dinner parties.

I, on the other hand, suck at parties. I hate mingling and working a crowd like an 8-year-old hates Saturday morning chores. I'll worm out of those events every time I can.

Maybe I'll find out I was actually adopted. Wouldn't that just take the cake?

****

I didn't know a tremendous amount about my dad's childhood, which really is odd because of how many years I lived with him and his parents. My dad was the only child of Era and Elton Sanders, Nana and Pop to us. Because we didn't have uncles or aunts to tell stories, we never heard much about him being a boy. Oh, we'd hear the occasional story, like the time he put hydrogen peroxide on his hair to get the summer blonde look. Instead, he got the summer blistered head look. And his hair didn't turn blonde; it turned loose. And it didn't come back. Chalk that one up to lesson learned the hard way.

And I heard that he was quite an athlete, but more by others than by him. In fact, I don't know anyone who talks about his or her achievements on the field as little as Dad does. There's not a specific story I can remember him telling me about his baseball or football days other than the self-effacing ones involving him not being able to hit a dominant curve ball.

Why is that? Why was his backstory as much of a mystery to me as my backstory?

So in researching for the book, I turned to Dr. Dee (Harden) Terry. Dee is one of my dad's three first cousins, along with Mickey and Bill Harden. Their mother, Doe Harden, was

Nana's younger sister. And while she was my great aunt, she was more like the fun aunt who's house you always enjoyed going to.

Nana's older sister, Eva was married to Pete. Their house was more stoic and less welcoming. Dad and Mickey found that out early on. While visiting Aunt Eva and Uncle Pete, Dad, 12 at the time and Mickey, 9, decided it would be fun to pull the emergency brake off of Aunt Eva's new Hudson Hornet, I guess, just to see what happened.

What happened is as follows:

The car rolled down the driveway, across the street and into a neighbor's garage, damaging both. Dad and Mickey's behinds were damaged by Uncle Pete. Said behind were later damaged by Aunt Doe. And those behind, along with the rest of their bodies, were summarily banned from visiting Aunt Eva and Uncle Pete's house at the same time. By themselves, Aunt Eva and Uncle Pete determined, they were fine boys. Together, they were mischievous hellions.

Who knew so many bad things could happen from pulling one emergency brake? After this day, I can tell you two men, both now in his 70s, who know.

I needed to learn stories like that about my dad. It shows a fun harmless but rebellious and adventurous streak in his youth that I knew nothing about. This tale notwithstanding, and because of the absence of anecdotes to the contraire, I've always assumed Dad's childhood was close to idyllic.

But, of course, every child grows up with a measure of crap around him or her. Every child – at least in part – is a product of his or her environment. The parents' wounds or accomplishments; mental disorders or stability that surpasses understanding; love or abuse, it all shapes the grownups we become.

Ask my dad if he had a good childhood and good parents, the quick answer, every time, would be yes. But no one escapes childhood unscathed.

The reality is, Dad grew up with an emotionally demanding and manipulative mother who employed guilt like she had a doctorate in it and sought out pity like a drunk seeks the bottle. I didn't know this for 40 years, but it all adds up. And it begins filling in some of the genetic backstory of who Dad is, who I am, who Rachel is.

Physically, Nana was never the picture of health. She had double pneumonia when Dad was a child. Then later in life, she was in a horrific car wreck that resulted in multiple broken bones – 144 if she is to believed. The human body has 206 bones. I doubt if the crash broke 70 percent of her bones in her body. Perhaps, and even this sounds a stretch, she had 144 breaks, if many bones were broken in five or six places.

I do know the crash was serious and she was hospitalized for a couple of weeks. But she complained of a bad heart, diverticulitis, failing organs and cancer. She did have a pre-cancerous lump taking off her scalp when she was in her 70s. But she had convinced my Dad from the time he was 10 years old that she was going to die any day.

She didn't really think that, but she wanted Dad to think that. And he did. All the time. She wanted to keep people emotionally and physically where she wanted them. Dad thinks maybe that's why he's not as compassionate as he should be.

I disagree with that. Dad's compassion tank has never been on empty. But him telling me he worried his mom was going to die all the time speaks volumes. Many kids grow up knowing their mom is going to die--from cancer or heart disease or some other terminal condition. To say that's no way to grow up, while obvious, feels a little disrespectful to the surviving offspring.

But having that fear for no reason other than control and to keep tight rein on emotional strings, is unequivocally no way to grow up.

Pop was the voice of reason in Dad's childhood. Like most in that generation, he worked Dad hard on Saturday mornings, took him to church on Sundays and demonstrated the work ethic of a man's man. While he tolerated Nana's ways with perseverance, he never gave weight to her foolishness. Maybe he was the only one in the house who didn't think Nana was about to die from the time she was 35.

For what it's worth, Nana died at 86 years old, essentially from old age.

Not long before she died, while in the hospital, she got mad because Pop had the nerve to leave her side for a few hours. She called 911 to report the emergency that she'd been left alone and was very sick. I guess it's not the only time anyone has ever called 911 while being an inpatient at a hospital. But it has to be rare. Welcome to the world of Nana.

In fairness, shortly after that, doctors finally prescribed her an antidepressant. It was the first time many of us had seen Nana carry on an unselfish, non-manipulative conversation. A few weeks later, Nana died. Still, it was nice for us to experience that side of her, even if it was in her final days.

When Dad began excelling at high school football, he would plead with Pop to figure out a way to keep Nana at home on game days.

"If I get hurt, she'd come running down to the field and would be in the coach's office after the game," Dad said. "Maybe she figured I was going to die, too, but usually, it was an ankle or knee."

Pop understood and worked with my dad to keep Nana away from the football field most of the time.

He'd modeled staying for my dad for 18 years. Back in the 40s and 50s, divorce was uncommon. Who knows if he'd have stayed with Nana in a different day and time. But Dad needed him to stay, almost as much as I needed him to stay. By doing the simple things like Nana away from his football games, he was creating a shame-free environment for Dad. That was a form of "staying."

By not getting frenzied when Nana was creating cause for it, by staying calm, Pop showed Dad that things were not spiraling out of control. By not letting my dad grow up thinking he could get away with disrespecting this flawed mom of his, Pop stayed and modeled respect.

These things kept my dad from resenting Nana. More importantly, it allowed his inner mettle to develop and become strong. He'd need that. We'd need that.

Dad left for college in the fall of 1958. And almost immediately, the only son had dozens of brothers.

To him, the Alpha Tau Omega fraternity taught him more life lessons than he learned in the University of Georgia School of Journalism. One thing my dad does not do better than me is putting subjects and predicates together. Among his many strengths, his writing indicates knowing where a comma should go is not one of them. He failed English 101 – twice. That's usually a pretty good indicator that a journalism degree might not be for you. But he got one anyway, which just shows how good he was at selling himself and convincing others to like him.

By 1960, he thought he was in love with a girl named Shirley. They dated for a year or so, he pinned her, and thought she might be the one for him. But first loves don't always last and

Dad and Shirley went separate ways. On the rebound, Dad met a good-looking freshman at an ATO party named Charlotte Burns.

Less than 18 months after going to college, after finally getting out from under a mother whose worse character flaw was her sick need to manipulate my dad, he fell for Charlotte. Freudian theorist would have a field day, and I'd be hard pressed to argue.

Dad says the primary concern he had after dating her for a few months was whether he could live up to her socialite expectations. She expected that from a boyfriend and especially if he was going to be considered husband-worthy.

It wasn't only that Dad was worried about whether he could provide such a life for her, he was pretty sure he didn't want to try. A year into the relationship, Dad gave serious thought to breaking up with Charlotte and trying to rekindle a romance with Shirley. Their relationship had ended a little more than a year earlier, and the breakup was cordial.

But two things prevented Dad from getting back together with Shirley: First, she was sending signals that she had emotionally moved on. But that paled in comparison to reason No. 2: Charlotte was pregnant.

Dad, like Cindy and me, was raised in the church and believed that premarital sex wasn't what God had in mind for us.

But life happens. Much more important than wallowing in the mistake of having premarital sex was what kind of man he was going to be in the wake of finding out he was going to be a father. The dad of The Great Stayer, turns out, was the original Stayer.

Charlotte and Dad were married by a justice of the peace in 1961. Dad took classes from 9 a.m. to 3 p.m., and then worked 4 p.m. to midnight at St. Mary's Hospital, calling people to remind them of their late payments during the first half of his shift, then cleaning up after patients during the second half.

This honeymoon-from-hell turned out to be the best phase of Dad's doomed marriage. But on August 16, 1962, little Cindy Sanders came into the world and quickly became his world. Three years later, I was added to the picture. Unhappy in marriage, we were the only reason Dad stayed with Charlotte. By the time I was born, if not well before, he knew Charlotte was not the kind of mother he could risk having primary custody of the two things that mattered most to him.

****

After college, Dad went directly into sales and rose through the ranks of a few companies before ultimately starting his own business in the mid 80s. As co-owner of an aluminum products company, he saw the best of financial times and, when the economy went south, the worst. But he had good business sense, and while he was not stingy, he placed a high value on money management. So the lean years were always manageable because of his frugality during the boon years.

I learned a lot from my dad, but usually when he wasn't trying to teach me. I learned about staying from him. I learned how to treat a lady from him. And I learned the value of a firm handshake and looking a grownup in the eye and addressing him or her with respect.

But if learning were based solely on the amount of times I heard something from him, the most-treasured nugget of knowledge would have been: "Birds of a feather flock together." I understood what that meant from the first time I heard it, simply because I was not a moron and he was not trying to disguise his message.

"Do not hang out with the wrong crowd because you'll be guilty by association," he'd tell Cindy and me.

Gotcha, Dad.

And it wasn't what you know, but who. That was a big one with him, and it seemed to fly in the face of his "study hard and make good grades" speech. But he managed to preach both on a single night without ever seeing a contradiction. When I got old enough to start thinking for myself, and became a tad bit socially conscious, I'd argue the whole "it's not what you know, it's who" thing with him. It just didn't seem right or noble or fair to me. I've yet to win an argument with him, though.

Oh, and about that fairness thing: "Life's not fair. You'd rather be lucky than good. And take every unfair advantage you can get." Those rounded out the greatest hits of his repertoire.

So...If I were to have learned only the lessons he was trying to teach, I'd have only associated with the movers and shakers (who never really seemed to like me) and I would've relied on luck, cut corners to out-manipulate my friends, turned up my nose at the sinners of the world and grown up using way more clichés than I already do.

So I suppose I learned most from his example, not his sayings.

One thing he had no clichés for was his desire for us to keep our bedrooms neat and orderly. Turns out, no clichés means he meant business.

I wasn't particularly good at keeping him happy on that front. He was much like a ticking bomb on room cleanliness (pardon the cliché). Twenty-nine days out of the month, pretty good was good enough. Pretty sloppy would earn us a polite reminder to go straighten up. But every so often--he'd lose his ever-loving crap. Suddenly he was Jack Nicholson in The Shining. He'd throw jackets, pull poorly folded clothes out of the drawers and start doing it the right way, while in the throes of a tear-inducing lecture. Those nights were my Dad at his worst, seeking to embarrass and shame me into being a better room-cleaning son.

Instead, it gave me a reason to fear him, to flinch when he came into my room, and to remember those times vividly these 35 years later.

God said:

Your dad had a rough go of it, but you know that. He learned well from Pop and you learned well from both of them. I was there, taking care of your Dad's heart when Nana was scaring him. I was there too when he met Charlotte. And I was there when he impregnated her. It's important that you realize that. You've heard your whole life that I am omnipresent, always there. This is what that means. I didn't turn away. It broke my heart when he sinned; it breaks my heart when you sin. But I don't turn away. Ever. I don't blink. I stay.

And Nana? She was a piece of work, wasn't she? I cannot wait for you to meet the real Nana, the one without disease and insecurities and the heaviness of life. She is a favorite of mine. And yeah, I say that about them all. And I'm right. You'll see in time.

Chapter 8 – A New Mom

*"The mother of the lad said, "As the Lord lives
and as you yourself live, I will not leave you."*
– Kings 4:30

"You get one mother. Deal with it."
– The Deceiver

On August 20, 1976, I got a new mom.

I hesitate to use the word "new" because to me, it seemed like I was finally getting my first mom. Equally important, I was getting something else that I had longed for – a new normal.

Dad met Lucy at work in 1974 in Orlando. She was 24 years old, recently divorced and had a 1-year-old daughter.

The first time they met, Lucy saw something in Dad that intrigued her. She saw a sense of humor, a contagious smile and his sweet, generous spirit.

She also saw a ridiculous toupee. Dad was "folliclely" challenged from the time he legally had his first beer.

Now don't get me wrong; I'm a firm believer that bald or mostly bald men can be devastatingly handsome and appealing to the fairer sex. (Yes, I inherited that gene from Dad.) But c'mon. This toupee, a big, brown hairy scalp cap that some of the cheesier and more-desperate men in the early '70s wore, couldn't fool a grown woman with sight, right?

Cindy and I had seen this hairpiece before. We might have been too young to judge for certain, but it didn't look real to us. I was 8 years old, when he first got it and I remember wondering: "OK, so suppose the wig somehow tricks the woman. That's fine for the first date and maybe the second. But what happens when the inevitable moment arises? (Of course, the inevitable moment to an 8-year-old is something like an urge to jump into a swimming pool.)

"But still Dad," I remember thinking. "How are you going to handle that one, big fella?"

Anyway, the first time Lucy saw Dad she was subbing at the front receptionist desk. Dad walked in the office wearing the toupee. Lucy was convinced right away: Now, there's a man with a good sense of humor!

In fairness, I suppose he might have been playing a joke on someone, like Lucy had assumed. But he didn't buy the rug as a joke. He bought it when he became single again for the same reason every other rug-buyer did, to look younger and better.

To me, he didn't look younger and better. He looked liked Mr. Carlin from the old Bob Newhart Show. And while I liked the TV show, I didn't want Mr. Carlin for a dad.

Regardless, Lucy found my dad to be charming, easygoing and someone who laughed a lot. And just like Dad, she needed someone with those traits.

It didn't take long for Dad and Lucy to fall in love. And on August 20, 1976, at Morningside Baptist Church in Atlanta, just a few miles from the house from which I stolen, I was getting a mom.

The wedding was small and simple, with no bridesmaids or groomsmen. Lucy had a more formal wedding in her first marriage and didn't want another. That was fine with Dad, who'd had a justice-of-the peace wedding in what now seemed to him like a lifetime ago.

Dad stood alone with the Rev. Jim Westbury – the Morningside Baptist Church pastor who had come to court in Dad's defense five years earlier – until Lucy made her way down the isle. The simple, but pretty "church dress" fit the moment. Neither wanted anything more than to start a new life and a new family with each other.

With Lucy in place, Dr. Westbury asked Dad to repeat after him.

"I Bill Sanders, take Lucy Lumley to be my lawfully wedded wife, in good times and in bad, in sickness and in health, till death do us part."

Dad repeated those words, just as the preacher had asked.

Dr. Westbury then asked Lucy to repeat after him.

"I Lucy Lumley take Bill Sanders to be my lawfully wedded husband, in good times and in bad, in sickness and in health, till death do us part."

She repeated those words, kind of.

Instead of doing it perfectly, her nerves got the better of her for a tenth of second and she said, "In thickness and in health." (It really helps to say it out loud for effect.) Maybe she got nervous because behind the preacher's back, Amy, her 2-year-old daughter, had taken off on an exploration of the choir loft and the organ chamber. Had Dr. Westbury seen Amy, he'd have probably stopped the service long enough for an adult in the congregation to corral Amy. But he didn't, and no one did any corralling.

That Amy didn't somehow fall and bring down something of significance, reverence or expense with her, meant that in "thickness and in health" wound up being the thing that we'd still laugh about almost 40 years later, whenever there's a family gatherings and someone's tongue gets tied. Had Amy been a tad bit more mischievous, who knows what the stories would have survived the years.

A few hours after getting a mom, I threw up.

Yes, my new life was being christened in the bathroom with heaves and a steady stream of onion dip and punch coming back up. I think it had little to do with nerves and lots to do with over-indulging at the reception.

After their short honeymoon, Dad, Cindy, me, my new mom and Amy, all moved into our new house in Marietta. Nana and Pop stayed in their midtown home. For the first time in seven years, I was living apart from my grandparents. Over those seven years, I'd spent more time with Nana and Pop than I had with my Dad. Much more.

But I was good with this. I liked my new mom, maybe even loved her. I'm not sure at the time that I did, but if not, I grew to quickly. And I could get used to not being the baby of the family, too. Even in the midst of some dark times that were still surrounding me, there was a lightness about this new normal that was so needed, so welcomed.

Still, for anyone paying attention, this new Sanders crew was quite the sight:

Mom, who was now 26 years old, slender and had long black hair down to her waist, was suddenly in charge of:

- Cindy, who was 14, starting her freshman year at a new high school.

- Me, 11, preparing to start sixth grade and puberty.

- Amy, about to turn 3, and a bit of a hellion.

84 | *STAYING*

Dad? Oh, he was still on the road on most weeknights, where the living was, well, maybe not easy, but a lot quieter. What could possibly go wrong?

****

Our new mom was learning on the fly, of course.

She thought everything was going to be a fairy tale, with all of us living happily ever after. To this day, she'll say it was fairly idyllic. Her first marriage hadn't been good either, obviously, seeing as how it ended. She had always wanted a family like this. We all did.

We had our own little fairly tale theme going on at the kitchen dinner table, particularly when Dad was gone and it was just us kids. (Remember, this new mom of mine was in her mid 20s.) We were all silly enough at the dinner table that we imagined once that people would hide in the woods and watch us eat dinner. Not in a creepy way, but in a sitcom way. It's pretty hard now to picture that in anything but a psychological thriller way. But remember, we'd all come from our own traumas, so perhaps our sense of humor was a bit on the odd side. Besides, our stories not withstanding, those really were slightly more innocent times.

Cindy and Mom had contests to see who could burp the loudest and longest. Mom was really good. Cindy could have gone pro. That always made us laugh. Then when we started laughing, someone would show the others what see-food looked like. Then

Amy would do something that a three-year-old does and Mom would get flustered and Cindy and I would egg her on.

Innocently enough, one of us, I think it was Mom, said our dinnertime hijinks was worthy of an *I Love Lucy* episode, or more likely *Three's Company*, with a lot of physical comedy. She said, "What would people think if they saw us acting this way from outside the window, but didn't know how normal we were?"

We laughed even more. Whenever Dad wasn't home, if everyone was in a good mood, we put on a pretty good show for our imaginary audience. Innocence. Pure goodness. Light.

But the post-dinnertime hours weren't always as light. On one of our first nights in our new home, Mom heard a noise downstairs. Dad was out of town (naturally) so Mom, fully in charge of our safety and security, did the only logical thing one would do when hearing a sound downstairs: She went into the closet and came out with my dad's shotgun.

I'm pretty sure she had no idea how to load or shoot the gun. And I'm guessing that she had never heard how new houses settle and make slight noises, particularly at night, when everything else is quiet.

No one had broken in; there was nothing to shoot. But I think we all might have slept in the master bedroom that night.

Fear was a common nighttime companion for all of us. Because of this, Cindy had been given strict orders to not see the movie *The Shining*. Of course, she was 17, so as far as movies were concerned, strict orders from her parents carried no weight. The thing is, Cindy didn't like scary movies. But her boyfriend at the time did.

Cindy told my parents not to worry, that they were going to see something else. Cindy lied.

And Cindy slept in a sleeping bag that night at the foot of my parents' bed, claiming her room was too hot – as if a sleeping bag was cooler.

At about 14, I had done the same thing with the book Amityville Horror, which to this day is the scariest thing I've ever read or seen. Of course, 14 year-olds tended to believe the claims that everything in that book was true. After one night of sleeping on my parents' floor – I don't think I made up any foolishness about it being too hot in my room – Mom decided to read the book, probably to tell me how silly I was acting.

Mom went to bed that night reciting The Lord's Prayer over and over, paying particular attention to "Deliver us from Evil." I didn't get a hard time about being spooked by that book anymore, either.

It wasn't too long into our new family structure that I had a sex education class in middle school. At 12, I knew way less about sex than probably most boys my age. I knew where babies came from – I think – but had little or no sense that there was any other reason for sex. Of course, what we taught in seventh grade in 1977 was high on biology and menstruation cycles, somewhat lower on anatomy, and very limited on sexuality.

I had never had 'the talk," and up till then and long afterwards, I had no need to have been given "the talk."

But I decided I'd ask some preliminary questions on the subject to my new Mom. Somehow, it seemed less embarrassing to talk to her about sex than it did with Dad. Thankfully, I don't remember a lot of what I asked or how she responded. In class, we had briefly talked about something called nocturnal emission, which is the one thing I remember asking Mom about.

She was a trooper about it. She hemmed and hawed a little, searching for the right way to address her puberty-stricken son she'd just inherited on, of all things, nocturnal emissions.

I didn't know what "nocturnal" was, nor did I know what "emissions" meant.

Whatever she said, I remember my response being, "Oh, it's like a wet dream?"

Wet dreams I had heard of. (Although I had not had one and assumed it was akin to wetting the bed. So to say I'd heard of them was the extent of what I knew about them.)

Confident that I now knew what a nocturnal emission was – so to speak – the impromptu sex-ed class ended, much I'm sure to her relief.

****

Despite my track records with moms, I never consciously worried about whether my new mom, this mom, would stay. I did, though, have a recurring dream that she and my dad had separated and that while I was never the cause of it, I was emotionally invested in fixing it. And in my dreams, I never saw my new mom as the villain. I don't think I saw Dad as the bad guy either, but I mostly wanted to fix things for her.

I guess a shrink would say this was a subconscious expression of me really fearing that my new mom would go away, whether on her own volition or not.

I cannot recall my dad ever saying anything bad about this new mom of mine. Almost 40 years later, I don't think I've heard him put her down or even talk down to her. And she loved my dad well, as far as I could tell, at all times. He has quirks, a few that I'm already seeing in myself and few more that are probably there but I'm not seeing them, that he inherited from Nana and that would challenge the mettle of a stayer. Over the last couple of years, as I've thought about this new name God has given me, I've began to see how that trait was modeled for me, not only by Dad, but by my mom.

She puts up with his Nana-risms, which are not easy to live with. Until the last few weeks of Nana's life, she and my mom did not like each other. To get a picture of their relationship, think of Debra Barone and mother-in-law Marie Barone, from Everybody Loves Raymond, and then subtract the laughs. Nana would talk about how second marriages rarely lasted. It sounds impossible, but I don't think she was saying that in a mean way. It was more of a warning not to get too attached to any woman other than her.

And now my mom is married to this man who, at 74, acts a lot like Nana. And she continues to not only stay, but to love him well.

God said:

You were fathered well. Eventually, you were mothered well. And I was your counselor, therapist, sounding board and guidance counselor all those years. There were lots of good therapists out there, and ideally, you and Cindy, and your dad, would have visited one. That wasn't afforded to you. But do you think I was going to let that stop Me from providing what you needed most? Not a chance. Remember, I knew how this was going to play out. Oh, and watch how much onion dip you eat at any given seating. It's as bad as there is when it's coming back up.

Chapter 9 – Loyalty

"There are 'friends' who destroy each other, but a real friend sticks closer than a brother."
– Proverbs 18:24

"How's that roster of friends looking for you?"
– The Deceiver

To Nana, I was "puh-fect" in every way. I think I might have mentioned that, but it was so true in her eyes, that it bears saying again. I never disappointed her. "Neva," she said in her heavy southern drawl.

Oh, I did plenty that would have disappointed Nana had she been even remotely aware that I was not perfect in every way.

When I was about 12, my best friend, Jimmy Powell and I decided we were going to purchase a Penthouse magazine – the one with Donna Summers on the cover – and we were smart enough to pull it off it right under Nana's nose.

Remember that bit about puberty? Well, the budding testosterone was going to outdo the shrinking common sense. But I was also going to learn a little about loyalty that afternoon, which is a key characteristic of a stayer.

Was our plan foolproof? The better question was: Was our plan so riddled with holes that even a bespectacled granny could see right through it?

Anyway, here's how Operation See Naked Women went down. We would ditch Nana and Pop (Pop loved me as much as Nana, but saw me for who I was, which was a hormone-crazed preteen. But that didn't seem to bother him) and tell them we were going into the bookstore to buy a baseball magazine or two.

That part of the plan really was solid and believable. Jimmy, now the Braves radio announcer, and I loved baseball and football. When we weren't playing them, we were talking about them. Or reading about them. Or watching them.

Nana had no reason to be suspicious during the five minutes that it should have taken us to walk to the magazine rack, choose between a handful of options, pay the lady at the cash register and meet her in front of Waldenbooks inside the mall.

I'm here to tell you this: Unless you have ice water in your veins, buying your first Penthouse magazine, when you are 12, is not a five-minute job.

We first had to ask the cashier if she would sell us one. Somehow, in the negotiation phase of Operation See Naked Women, we decided that one of us would ask the cashier if we could buy one, and then the other one would buy it – spreading the risk equally, or at least spreading the embarrassment. It took us a good 10 minutes just to agree that one would do one part of the job, and the other would do the other job. (If anyone was paying attention to us, it had to be hysterical.)

Jimmy quickly jumped in front of me and uttered the words, "Ma'am, can we buy any of the magazines off the rack?"

"Hmm. I guess so. But what do your mamas think?" she said. (Buying porn in 1977 apparently was legal for a kid. But man, was it hard.)

Anyway, Jimmy had done his job, the little weasel. That meant I had to fulfill my role, which was by far the more difficult part.

Standing on my tiptoes, I grabbed the Penthouse magazine off the top rack and quickly folded it lengthwise, so the back of the magazine was visible to the nosy public. I then began the longest walk ever, from rack to cashier. Seriously, how could a mall bookstore be the equivalent of 1.3 miles?

I walked past a gauntlet of disapproving little old ladies, probably nuns out of uniform. I walked past the religious aisles, where 200 different versions of the Bible sprouted eyes and glared at me, disgustedly. With a sweaty brow, trembling hands and a shaky voice, I finally got to the cashier.

"Is this all?"

"Yes, ma'am."

The ma'am part is important for you to know. Because even though I felt like the most shameful boy in the world right then, by God, I had my good manners to fall back on.

I dug into my jeans pocket and pulled out a five-dollar bill for two magazines. One was every boy's Holy Grail, the other was a Sports Illustrated, or Sporting News, or something with sports in the title. Only one magazine mattered. The other was its camouflage.

The totality of our ingenuity could be boiled down to this: We'd slide the Penthouse inside the sports magazine, just in case you could see through the bag. Brilliant, right? And well worth the 40 minutes it took us to pull this off.

As it turned out, you couldn't see through the bag. And as it turned out, that didn't matter.

Neither of us had considered this Nana woman might, just might, be able to muster up a little suspicion. I don't think it was really me she was worried about. After all, I was perfect. But Jimmy? He was s little devil who couldn't be trusted.

So right there, inside the mall, walking towards Rich's Department store, Nana demanded to see what was in the bag. Jimmy carefully took out the magazines to show her there was only one, and it was a sports magazine. But we didn't want to look at it here, we told her. We wanted to wait to get home and unfold all the exciting stats and player profiles.

Seriously. That's what we said.

What happened next is a blur, but within seconds, Nana was standing in the middle of the mall, holding a Penthouse magazine in her right arm, which was extended high in the air.

"What. Is. This?" she asked.

Now that was an embarrassing question on so many fronts. First, she really didn't know what she was waving around in public. She was the only one who didn't know, by the way. Secondly, that question gave us the tiniest of openings to continue the lie and likely extend our misery. Or, we could come clean, confess and start the healing.

Of course, we chose the lie.

Only thing is, we chose different lies.

"It's an entertainment magazine," Jimmy said. "You know, music, rock, Donna Summers?"

Simultaneously, I was feigning disgust, having chosen the never-successful We-Are-the-Victims route.

"Gross, how'd that get in our Sports Illustrated?" I hollered.

Poor Pop. Here was Nana, causing a scene, and here I was covering up and doing such an awful, awful job at it. There he was, wishing he could be anywhere else on earth. Nana, convinced we had shoplifted the magazine, made us go back to the bookstore, walk back to the smarmy cashier, and with her standing between Jimmy and me, asked her whether we had paid for this smut.

"Not only did they buy it, they didn't wait for their change or receipt. And they said their moms wouldn't mind," the cashier said with a smirk.

The Penthouse went in the trashcan.

And in what seemed like about 100 hours later, that day finally ended.

It would have been tricky, but Jimmy could have bailed on me that afternoon and stood back and let this play out within the family boundaries. He certainly didn't have to stand there, making up excuses and absorbing some of the embarrassment like he did.

And while I don't see how I could have bailed on him in that moment, I was encouraged to do just that the next morning, after we'd taken Jimmy home.

I wouldn't do it though. At the time, I didn't see it as heroic. And based on our lame attempts at lying our way out of trouble, I clearly wasn't above a little white lie that would have cleared my reputation with Nana. I think part of me relished the recently earned reputation as a bit of a bad boy. But mostly, I didn't like it when Nana and Pop, or my dad even, would talk about Jimmy like he was less than trustworthy. He was, and still is, the picture of trustworthy, and introduced me to loyalty.

I'd soon come to value loyalty above just about any other trait. And I'd become acutely aware of when I was seeing it in others and when I wasn't. Acutely aware would morph into obsessively aware. And if you pay obsessive attention to who is fiercely loyal to you and who is not, you'll be disappointed over and over. And you'll wonder why everyone leaves, why nothing ends well, why good relationships die slow deaths.

At least I did.

My quest to find loyalty, people who will stay for the good and the bad, results in me labeling friends and even relatives as loyal or disloyal. And eventually, they all find their way to the latter list.

I know this is no way to live a fulfilled, God-centered life, but it's how I live most of the time. I'm not consciously labeling people. In fact, the vast majority of people, I have no expectations of. Mentally, draw a small circle and write the names of your immediate family, plus one or two of your closest friends. That circle can and will hurt you, let you down, frustrate you and make you the angriest, right? Because they are the one we love the most, they are the ones we have the strongest feelings toward and often spend the most time with. At least in my life, these aren't the ones in which I doubt loyalty.

It's the next circle out that wrecks me. Neighbors. Softball coaches. Fellow church members. Pastors. Colleagues. I don't put expectations on most people in any of those categories. But my circle would include probably 15 to 20 people who I genuinely care about, who's heart I have fought for and who I've risked vulnerability with. The circle after that contains names of folks from those categories – people I may come in contact with daily – but people who cannot hurt me simply by walking away or abandoning the relationship.

I guess I hold the circle with the 15 or 20 people in it to a ridiculously high standard, because every one of them has disappointed me because, in my eyes, they haven't cared for me the way I care for them. I am convinced that given time, I will cause everyone in this circle to leave me because they will grow exhausted of trying to live up to my expectations of them, even though I think I keep those to myself.

Even as I write this, I understand how petty, insecure and self-absorbed that sounds. I'll cop a plea to being insecure most of the time, petty some of the time and self-absorbed a little of the time. I have handed those traits down to both of my children, I'm afraid. Sins of the father? I guess. Genetic predisposition to want to please? Probably.

Then I'm reminded that even in all of these things, maybe because of them, I am more than a conqueror. He is strong when I am weak. Pettiness or insecurity has not and will not separate me from the love of God. And his grace has been and will be sufficient.

Besides, none of those traits are the truest things about me.

I am a joint heir with Jesus. He doesn't just love me; he delights in me. He created me to be the guy that I am, not some better, less-annoying me. This me.

So not everyone has stayed. My inner-circle isn't huge. So what? Whose is?

Eddie Vedder and Pearl Jam put it this way: "Oh, I'm a lucky man, to count on both hands the ones I love. Some folks just have one, yeah, others, they've got none, yeah. Stay with me. Let's just breathe."

Truth trumps fear. Courage is not denying that any of these nagging traits exist. It's knowing that while they do, and they do in every single one of us, they don't define us. Seeking loyalty, risking getting hurt and not masking the real me to make me look like someone better than I am put me in vulnerable state.

Author, speaker and researcher Brené Brows says: "The word I use to describe people who can live from a place of vulnerability is *wholehearted*... (Vulnerability) is the birthplace of joy, belonging, creativity, authenticity, and love."

This quest is universal. We might as well recognize it, talk about it and be encouraged that it's not only a survivable state. It's a holy one.

God said:

First, Poor Pop, indeed.

And as for people? They'll let you down. Often. And that includes the ones you love the most. Just stay though. Just breathe. There is One who is loyal all the time. One who would die for you and who could save you by doing just that. Look to Me, and only me, to satisfy that need in your life. No one else is built to be able to meet that need. Expecting them to is not fair to them and not helpful for you. Living wholeheartedly though is helpful, to you and to those around you. I'm proud of this risky behavior of yours. Don't back down from vulnerability, and don't put back on the masks that hide the imperfections and weaknesses. Remember the song you sang to yourself over and over to go to sleep? 'We are weak, but He is strong.' It's true, ya know?

Chapter 10 – Terrors

"For the Lord GOD will help me; therefore shall I not be confounded: therefore have I set my face like a flint, and I know that I shall not be ashamed." – Isaiah 50:7

"You were, are, and always will be a coward." – The Deceiver

It's one thing for a kid to hide and seek cover when a Penthouse magazine was about to be waved in front of God and man... and innocent shoppers. I mean, c'mon. What kid wouldn't lie then?

But to turn that – not so much the lying, but the hiding – into an art form that played out every day was an exhausting, humiliating task.

I was either in sixth or seventh grade the first time I remember being picked on in school. There was nothing unique about my appearance or mannerisms. I was average height and weight, with a slightly goofy, bowl-shaped haircut with bangs down to my eyebrows. I wore clothes like the other kids wore, could talk about sports with the best of them and could play sports at what was at least an average level.

My most visible quirk was that my feet turned out when I walked, like a duck. Oddly, I don't remember that being a source of much pain or ridicule. But I wore a sign around my neck that said: "I can be victimized. Easily. I won't stand up for myself."

Every day of middle school and high school, I'd get up, eat breakfast, get dressed, put that sign around my neck and walk to school.

It had been engrained in me that I was a victim, that I needed be taken care of and that I did not have what it took.

So I'd get bullied, usually verbally, by boys who were smaller than me, bigger than me, uglier than me, smarter than me and dumber than me.

I was an equal opportunity target.

If I'm being fair, I probably experienced direct bullying maybe only a dozen or so times a year – maybe not even that many. And there were plenty of kids who had it worse than me.

But 12 times a year multiplied by six years might as well amount to every single day. That's because the nine days out of 10 that I wasn't picked on, I lived anticipating being picked on. I can honestly say I do not remember a single carefree day of middle or high school.

I would have done just about anything to work my way out of this cycle except for the one thing that was essential: Standing up for myself.

I'd negotiate, placate, facilitate. I'd try to mimic the way the cool kids stood or walked or talked. And then someone would come up behind me and knock my books out of my hand, sending papers sprawling all over the crowded halls. Then the kid would say something akin to, "What are you gonna do about it?"

What was I gonna do about it? Now that was a stupid question. I was gonna do the same thing I did every other time. Nothing. Hope the moment would pass without further embarrassment and hope I didn't get punched in the face.

Every time my notebook was knocked out of my hands from behind, it wasn't just the months' worth of sloppily crammed-in syllabi that were scattered and now being trampled upon beneath the feet of kids going from one class to another. No, that I could have lived with. It was hope getting shoved to the ground, getting trampled on and scattered about, minimized and trivialized. Those are the things I could never pick up and jam back into place. Instead, as I bent over to pick up the dirty, shoe-print smudged, loose-leaf papers, wondering why no one ever stopped to helped me, shame would hop on my back. I'd stand back up feeling six inches shorter and weighted down by then nameless spirit of shame.

I felt alone as I faced, or failed to face, the bullies and the shame. I felt abandoned by God and by friends, and because I was too embarrassed to speak of it to my dad, I essentially made the decision for him that he'd abandon the situation by not knowing it existed.

I wish I could back in time for about 30 seconds and have a talk with the 10-year-old me. It might not be the same thing God would say, so it's probably just as well.

Here's what I would tell the 10-year-old me:

"Punch some kids in the face. In fact, pretty quickly you're going to need to do that or it's going to be too late. In fact, make a habit of doing it once or twice a year. Any more than that, you'll be a troublemaker. Much less than that, you'll not know how to stand up for yourself. In fact, find someone else getting picked on, walk right into the middle of it, and smack the bully. Here's a tip no other 10-year-old is gonna get. Use the outside fleshy part of the first, the part you'd use to break a board in Karate class, except make a fist.

"You won't like punching someone, which is good. And you won't like getting smacked back either. But neither are things to avoid at all cost."

****

I did not going out for the football team, mainly, because I didn't know how to put shoulders pads on. And screwing that up, in a locker room, would be like throwing red meat to a lion. I'd have no part of that. So I showed them all by never playing a sport I liked and was probably pretty good at.

Instead, I'd walk home after school and shoot baskets in my driveway, either by myself or with one of the kids in my neighborhood. There were four or five kids my age that lived on my block. I felt comfortable in my neighborhood – more so there than any other place. I wasn't picked on, I fit in and I didn't have to pretend to be something more than I was.

On Mother's Day afternoon, 1980, while shooting baskets, a car pulled up to the curb by our mailbox. Charlotte stepped out of the car. It was the first time I'd laid eyes on her since I had been snatched out that car window in 1971.

"I just wanted you to see who your REAL mother was," Charlotte said.

How did she know where we lived? How had she found the one place where I felt at ease?

"I just wanted you to see who your real mother was," might as well have been "I stole you once; I can do it again."

Having uttered one sentence, she got back in the passenger seat of the car and drove off.

On a conscious level, I don't remember that drive-by as being horribly traumatic. But I had no read on my subconscious psyche.

I was still ritualistically rolling my head back and forth to go to sleep. If I fell asleep within 20 or 30 minutes of turning off the lights, it was going to be a good night. If I lay in bed for 30 minutes or more, I'd start worrying. I did not want to be the last one awake in the house. And with every tick of the clock, that was closer to being my reality for the night.

I would look out my door, down the hall, to see if my parents' lights were still on. Their door was shut, which was fine by me. As long as I could see light coming out from the crack underneath the door, I was fine. Often, the bright light became a dim blue light. That meant the lights were out, but the TV was still on. That was my 15-minute warning.

Gotta fall asleep, now. Roll my head a little harder to drown all the rest of the world and exhaust myself a little more.

Every night, I'd pray to Jesus, "Please help me go to sleep without any problems. Once the blue light was extinguished, the prayers unanswered that night, I'd nervously lie in bed, knowing that eventually, exhaustion would win.

On a scale of 1 to 10, on the nights when my dad was in town, my normal nighttime anxiety would start at a 3 and go up a notch every 15 minutes or so I was awake. When my dad was out of town, and my stepmom was in charge, it would start at about a 6.

From the age of 11 to maybe 15, about once every other month or so, I'd go into their room and sleep on the floor. Other than those occasions, I'm certain my dad, and the woman who I have always called Mom, and whom I love like a mother, had no idea of my nighttime fears.

I was not afraid that Charlotte was going to come back and do something in the middle of the night. I was afraid some stranger would break into my house and take me.

I lived so much of my life afraid and embarrassed that I was afraid. I was not going to further the shame by telling anyone I was being bullied during the day and afraid at night. Feeling alone as a kid does something that changes the trajectory of our lives. For some, it makes a real connection unlikely. For others, right the opposite.

Maybe that's why I would check in on Rachel a half dozen times between when the lights went out and when she fell asleep, even in those few easy-sleeping years. It might have been a bit neurotic of me. But if my girl was going to feel afraid at night, she wasn't going to feel alone as well.

By the time I was in high school, the daytime and nighttime pattern continuing, I began to worry about what going to college would look like. I was pretty sure I didn't have what it took to make it on my own, though.

God said:

"I remember those nights well, Bill. I stood guard at your door. I allowed your parents to fall asleep with the TV on more than once, just to keep the blue light on for you. I hate fear. I don't want you, or any of my children, to live in it. I know you did, though. And it's not your fault. But again, I was determined I'd use

those fearful years in you. You wouldn't have understood then. But I was shaping the heart of Rachel's father. She was going to need you. She was going to need a tender heart that understood irrational fears. And she'd need a father who was strong enough to fight for her heart." And he was right.

****

A few weeks after Charlotte made her Mothers' Day appearance in front of my house, she and Claire showed up at Cindy's high school graduation, in early June of 1980, uninvited of course.

Cindy's graduating class was large and there was another high school finishing up graduation ceremonies while Cindy's class was assembling outside the Marietta Civic Center under a blazingly hot late morning sun.

Mom, Dad and I dropped Cindy off at the door and went to find a parking place. A lot happened in those five minutes.

"Surprise! Look who's here," Claire, with Charlotte at her side, said to Cindy. "Look at you! You look so much like your mother. Look at how much weight your mom has lost! Isn't she beautiful?" She's doing so much better now, too."

Charlotte didn't say much. She had a diamond ring that she said Mr. Burns had given her. She took it off and asked if she could put it on Cindy's finger. She took her hand, not waiting for an answer and put it on for her.

"Isn't that pretty?" Charlotte said.

Classmates watched; some of them giggled. Cindy never said a word.

The scene might have played out on it's own. I'm sure Charlotte and Claire knew their window for this was brief. And it was. As Dad, Mom and I were walking up the sidewalk toward the civic center, Dad spotted them and let out a disgusted, "Oh, Lord!"

"We're leaving, Bill," Claire said. "Charlotte wanted to give Cindy her ring. And she's doing much better by the way."

Charlotte didn't say anything this time.

Neither did I. Other than Dad's "Oh Lord," sigh, none of us said anything. Somehow, Charlotte could still stun us with her antics. And just like that, she disappeared again.

Cindy didn't go to any graduation parties that night. She stayed home, more numb than scared, she later would tell me. I stayed home too wondering when the next time Charlotte would appear.

She never did. In fact, I never saw Charlotte's face again.

For more than 20 years, none of us heard anything from Charlotte or Claire or the Burns. And that was more than fine with us.

But on February 11, 2002, Charlotte reached back into our world – more specifically, into Cindy's world. It was the same kind of subtle psychological game she'd played when she made her brief appearance in front of my house back when I was 15.

But it was creepier.

As far as any of us knew, Charlotte had lost track of us, or interest in us. And everyone was fine with that. So when Cindy got a letter, mailed to her house, Cindy's first question was the right one. "How does she know where I live?" Cindy asked.

When she started reading the note, a 30-year-old fear, which had been largely dormant, came to life like it had been revived with defibrillator paddles.

She not only knew where Cindy lived. She knew everything. She knew Cindy was married to Pat, who "is not too bad on the drums either, I hear," Charlotte wrote. "Christopher is so old; he seems to be thought of quite well."

Chris was 21 and a student at the University of Georgia.

"And Becky must be getting too, too grown up. What a blessing for you that your life has been a good one. (I hope). We just hear tidbits, here and there."

Becky was 17 and at a Roswell Street Baptist Church event when the letter arrived.

Charlotte, the letter said, had been brought up to speed on Cindy and her family by a family with whom she had placed a Yorkshire terrier. That family was a member of Roswell Street Baptist Church.

Cindy called Pat, and immediately they went to the church and stayed the rest of the day, not telling Becky that anything was up, but not willing to take any chances either.

The letter included an invitation to catch up, to "go forward from here. The Holy Spirit alone can guide both of us."

She signed it: "Your First Mama, Charlotte."

The letter mentioned me, in passing. It also mentioned that she had lung cancer.

Among the things not in the letter: An apology, an indication she was taking any responsibility, a hint of remorse.

Whether the letter was meant as a psychological attack, we'll never know. Was Becky in any danger at church that day? Probably not.

But you reap what you sow. Charlotte's benefit of the doubt had long since run out. We are left with the assumption that she abandons, manipulates, terrorizes and makes subtle threats. This is what she earned over the years. And it's what she was sowing.

It wasn't until I began investigating some details of Charlotte's life for this book that I learned she indeed did have lung cancer in 2002. She had been a smoker. If and when she quit, I don't know.

The cancer took her life on June 11, 2004. Sometimes, death certificates are enlightening. Charlotte's offered little.

She died from respiratory arrest following years of a metastatic, non-small cell lung cancer. At the time of her death, she was in the inpatient care of Hospice Atlanta, according to the death certificate. She was married and living in metro Atlanta. No autopsy was performed, and her body was cremated.

I've watched one person die from cancer. His didn't start in his lungs, but it made its way there. It was excruciating to watch as he gasped for air. There might be worse ways to die, but not many. I know I wouldn't wish it on my worst enemy.

I wouldn't have wished it on Charlotte, either.

But I'm not sure what I would have wished for her. Throughout the years, I didn't actively hate her. But I never actively forgave her, either.

God said:

I loved Charlotte. I hated what she did to you and to Cindy and to your dad, but I loved her. Always. I kept my arms open for her to coming running home, just like I have for you on more than one occasion. Charlotte had run away and done unthinkable things, just like the Prodigal Son. I suspect, had she come running to you and Cindy, you both would have forgiven her. You probably wouldn't have called for the fattened calf and thrown a party, but I think had I really impressed that on your heart, you would have. (And for the record, I wouldn't have asked that of you.) I'm not going to tell you more about Charlotte's heart, her relationship or lack of one with me. Not on this side of eternity, anyway.

Chapter 11 –

How to Kiss a Girl

"I trust in God's unfailing love forever and ever."
– Psalms 52:8

"The Great Stayer? You booted your friend Jimmy once you became a Christian. You are a hypocrite and you are not a stayer." – The Deceiver

While I had a level of fear and anxiety every night, and at least moments of it every day, I thought I had it pretty good. I didn't know how unusual my anxieties were or really whether what I experienced on a daily or nightly basis was strange at all.

I played outside in the neighborhood, hard, almost every day. Two-on-two touch football in the street. One-on-one basketball in the driveway. Tennis and swimming during summer days and kick the can on summer nights.

Jimmy and I remained close friends. He lived about 20 minutes from my house, so we couldn't just walk outside and play. But at least once or twice during the week, and at least one of the weekend days, he'd come to my house or I'd go to his.

And we'd compete like warriors. I was his best friend, and he was mine. But we loved to get the best of each other in any athletic endeavor, and we'd set up ridiculously long games of one-on-one basketball, like first one to 100 wins.

Or we'd play one-on-one football in the street. It's not easy to play one-on-one touch football. But we were creative. We figured out how to pass the ball to ourselves, made up rules that governed our sport and went at it.

But whiffle ball was our game of choice. We played hundreds of games in our years together, and we were similar in skill level. We'd play nine innings, and the score would be 12-10. Or 9-8. Or, if the wind was just right, 4-3.

That's how close we were.

Thus, I cannot explain how he won 299 times and I won once. It is uncanny. I thought I was competitive and fierce. But I couldn't beat this kid. Our basketball scores were 100-96. He'd usually win. Almost always. But he wasn't as dominant in that, or in football, as he was in whiffle ball.

It has been 32 years, give or take a year, since these games took place. But I will never forget the magical game where his whiffle ball streak ended.

We were visiting my grandparents' house. We'd play in their front yard. It was a smaller field than his house or mine. Cozy confines. Wrigley Field, if you will.

I was leading by one run going to the ninth.

I'd been there before, mind you. And crumbled. Many times.

Jimmy got an imaginary man or two on base, and I managed to get a couple of outs. Reggie Jackson came to the plate, the winning runs on base.

And on the first pitch, it happened. Jimmy popped it up to the pitcher/me.

Whiffle balls, as any man worth his salt knows, spin and float in ways that defy gravity. But I was locked in. And I was a good enough athlete that this ball was not going to hit the ground.

The home crowd (it was *my* grandparents' house, not his) was on its feet in uncontrollable joy. I settled underneath it, called off the other imaginary players and promptly got hit in the gut by a flying yellow whiffle ball bat.

Yep, Jimmy was a bit more competitive than me. The streak meant enough to him that he would hurl a plastic bat at me in hopes it would distract me, maybe bloody my nose, whatever.

True confession: I didn't catch the ball. I caught the bat.

Jimmy argued his case that had this been a real baseball game, the batter would have been tossed out of the game (Ya think?), but he would not have been called out. A pinch hitter would take his place.

Jimmy was a solid arguer, but even he couldn't passionately defend this claim. I had won. He knew it. The streak was over. And I only had 299 to go before I caught him.

****

And pretty soon, maybe a little later than I'd have liked, girls, at least some girls, began showing interest in me. This gave me something new to think about at night as opposed to worrying about what time my parents would fall asleep.

I was going to church regularly just as I had all my life. By the time I was 16, I was more interested in finding a girlfriend than Jesus. After all, I heard a lot of Jesus and the cross and my sin and how I needed to find a way to be fired up and sold out for the Lord.

In one ear and out the other. I had believed in Jesus and was baptized as a child, and that seemed good enough to me. But there were some really cute girls at church, and no one ever picked on me there. In fact, I was a borderline cool kid in this environment.

For those reasons, I decided to go to a weeklong youth camp at Covenant College in Chattanooga, Tennessee. There, I met two people who would love me well for the rest of my life.

One was Stan, who has been my closest friend for 30 years now. We've taught each other, over the years, how to navigate the rough, rocky roads of life that everyone encounters. He gets me, maybe more than anyone on earth.

The other was Jesus – the real Jesus.

Even though I had believed He existed since I was a child, and had prayed to Him, it was more like rubbing on a Genie bottle of crawling into Santa's lap. And I'd heard a lot about what this Jesus fellow didn't like – drinking, premarital sex, cursing, or us thinking about drinking, having premarital sex or cursing. Oh he loved us, I was taught. But he probably didn't like very many of us.

So I met the real Jesus in the summer of 1982 and accepted him as my savior.

The problem was this: I came face-to-face with the real Jesus (not literally, I didn't see him in a pile of pasta), fell in love with Him, but only knew one way to be a follower of His, and that was to mimic what I saw in other sold-out, committed Christians at church.

I learned to evangelize, how to look holy and to be pretty sure I was better than those who were not doing beach or door-to-door evangelizing and who were doing any of those things that Jesus didn't condone.

I quit hanging out with Jimmy, not because Jimmy was a bad kid, but because he didn't talk about Jesus a lot.

This real Jesus? He loved me all right, but not because of who I had become. I think He loved me in spite of who I had become.

Still, after the summer camp, I felt more in my element at church than anywhere else

I (finally) full-fledged kissed a girl, thanks to this church. Then, another one. Looks-wise, both were out of my league, which is every guy's goal. I'll tell you about Carol, she of my first kiss, later. You'll like her a lot.

The other one, number two on my fairly short list, was named Faye. At the time, I was pretty sure I loved Faye. I'd spent a year pursuing her and settling for being the dreaded "just-friends" guy. She was dating the quarterback at an across-town high school. When that went south, the door was open for me. It was prom season; I was a senior, she was a junior and we went to the same school. So we decided to go to prom together, still under the umbrella of "just friends."

She'd told me ahead of time that she wouldn't be dancing to any slow songs. Whatever. I didn't know how to dance anyway. But a couple of hours into it, she changed her mind. We danced to Boz Scaggs' *Love, Look What You've Done to Me*. We danced like a couple of fourth graders in an Arthur Murray dance class, with nary a body part touching. But still. It was a slow song, a good one at that, and it wasn't a bad three minutes at all.

A few weeks later, on a Sunday evening, after church – and of course, a trip out to a local Sunday night after-church hangout – I drove her home in my smokin' hot, rust-colored Ford Pinto. She told me to park in front of her house instead of driving up the driveway. She said she had something to say.

"I've been thinking about this for a while now," Faye said.

"Thinking about what, about why I pull into the driveway," I asked, mostly serious.

"I've been practicing this in front of the mirror, so let me tell you how I feel," she said.

"OK."

Holy crap! Something was about to happen here!

"I don't know if I'm in love with you," she said. "I love you, but I don't know if I'm in love, or will fall in love. But we should date and see."

To myself: "We should date? She might be in love with me? HO-LY CRAP! This is seriously good."

To her I said: "I think that sounds like a fine idea, Faye."

"Should we shake hands on it?" she asked coquettishly.

It was the most coquettish moment of our summer-long fling where everything above the neck was permissible, and everything below the neck was closed for business.

We made out right then and there. At that point in my life, it was the best moment I'd ever known. The kid who was left as a child, picked on throughout school, who rolled his head to go to sleep at night while humming Jesus Loves Me, was making out with the homecoming queen who I had placed on a pedestal long ago.

Over the course of our three months of dating, she taught me how to hold hands with a girl in a godly way – both when at the movies and when walking. I am so thankful to Faye for that lesson, because apparently, she – and perhaps, her mom – was the only one in the entire world to whom God had explained this godly hand-holding technique.

Faye, somehow, could wear the pants in the relationship while instructing me that it was my role to be the pants-wearer.

Whatever. She let me make out with her, and that clouded the ridiculous rule regimen she had set up for the two of us. I was leaving for college in a couple of months anyway.

Before I left for college, Faye ended our whirlwind romance. But she did it like a true gentleman.

For the next 20 years or so, my idea of what God wanted and expected from me looked a lot like what Faye had taught me that summer. I might have said something different, if asked directly, but I believed God was mad at me one day, pleased with me the next, then disappointed for a week at a time, then happy with me for six hours, then repulsed at the thoughts going through my mind.

I had made it an exhausting relationship, one which I tried to keep alive out of duty and effort and fear about what might happen if God perceived me turning my back on Him.

This is the way an employee views a tough, cranky and unpredictable boss. Come to think of it, it's the way many grow up viewing their father. I didn't, except during those occasional room-cleaning fits.

But that's not how God sees me. He never did. Even when I assumed he saw me as the slacker employee or good-for-nothing son, He was seeing me as his beloved, nothing less. There were never times when He loved me more, or delighted in me more. Who was I kidding thinking I had enough self-effort to please a perfect, holy God?

I'm going to jump ahead, but just for a second.

I learned this over a several-year period while reading authors such as John Eldredge, John Lynch and Dan Allender. They taught me I could read the Bible without these man-made filters that caused me to read everything with the assumption that it was full of "ought-to's."

With those lenses replaced by ones that allow me to consider and read it all through the lens of love, everything changed.

So I exorcised everything in my life that felt or looked like legalism. I walked out of a Baptist church when the pastor said, "If you don't like what I'm saying, there's the door," one too many times. I used the door and have not gone back to what I would consider a legalism church service in 10 years, with the exception of a funeral or two.

I was not going to let my kids grow up believing in this kind of Christianity. We were going to be all about His love and grace. I still believe it's all about His love and grace. I understand holiness and righteousness. But it's all about grace and love, or else I, and the lot of us, are doomed. Still, I was throwing out the baby with the bathwater – in a big way.

I'm glad I drained the dirty bathwater, but my all-or-nothing extremism on church in general, or for a while against the Baptist church specifically, wasn't helpful. It wasn't good for me, or my wife Jane, but it was particularly harmful for my daughters, Rachel and Laura.

We spent six years at Warren Baptist Church in Augusta, Ga., under the leadership of Dr. Frank Page, who later became the president of the Southern Baptist Convention. We loved Dr. Page and the church and never heard a message we interpreted as legalistic. When we moved to Atlanta, we missed Warren, Dr. Page and our church friends, and became too critical of the churches we tried.

We've since found a great one. But we, and our girls, missed out on some important years because we were unwilling to look at others with the grace we were proclaiming. Again, I'm resting on the truth that love covers a multitude of sins.

God said:

"It was all being used, my boy. You were making a mess out of living for Me, but I used it for good. Your moral striving, your attempts to be better than who you were, your vision of what it meant to follow me. They were exhausting, weren't they? And frustrating. And needless. But you know that now. I'm happy you aren't trying so hard now. That wasn't the Bill I created and loved since before time. That was Bill plus all his self-righteousness, which isn't nearly as good to be with as the Bill I made.

This Jimmy fella turned out all right, didn't he? Oh, and I've got every one of those whiffle ball games on Blue-Ray up here, including a blooper reel of Jimmy's blunders. We'll watch them all together. You won't believe how close you were to winning several other games.

And as for Faye? I love her, too. But I didn't like the whole hand-holding, holier-than-Me episode any more than you did. But it did help you see how silly those things can be. And it's not like you learned them overnight, either. So we'll cut her some slack.

"Lastly, as for throwing the baby out with the bathwater? Whatever. It's in the past. I'm all about your present and your future. I'm all about how you let Me love you and how you love others, not because you 'ought to,' but because it's who you are. And the way it flows out of you naturally? That is so, so cool."

Chapter 12 –

For Better or For Worse

"An excellent wife, who can find? For her worth is far above jewels. The heart of her husband trusts in her." – Proverbs 31:10-11a

"You think you've been a Godly husband? Please. A selfish one, a lazy one and in the end, those are the things that will matter." – The Deceiver

After being left by a non-stayer, I was raised by a spectacular stayer, even if he was never given that name. In my mind, Dad was the Original Stayer, at least in my immediate lineage.

But I married a true stayer, too, one who has been vital in helping me live out the name God gave me.

Before I married Jane, I'd never had dated anyone for more than three or four months. I think I might have broken up with one girl in college. And another one moved away before either of us had to end it. But mostly, girls figured out pretty quickly that I was a funny fellow, had a good heart, bad hair, and was great "best friend" material. Carol, my first girlfriend, was the first to decide this. She let me down beautifully' and she was right of course. We were not made for each other. She was made for Paul, whom she was married to for 25 years or so. Faye, the Godly hand-holder, was next. That one stung a little more, but she too was right. I wasn't made for her and she wasn't made for me.

That pattern played out a few more times in college. I always dated out of my league in the looks category. That too, I'm sure, played no small role in my streak of being the one let go instead of the one doing the letting go.

A therapist could easily look at this streak of being dumped and draw conclusions about my need to not be abandoned. Who am I to say they would be wrong? But I think they would be. I know that never once did I see it as another example of being abandoned. I never once thought, "First my mom left me, now a girlfriend is leaving me." But I do think how this played out gave me a longing for someone who believed in me enough, somehow saw past my thin, cow-licked hair, and thought my schtick was actually no schtick at all, but it was me being me, and that that was a enough.

Jane was the one to do all that. And turns out, she needed what I had to offer, as well.

We met while working for a small-town newspaper. She likes to tell people that she was my boss, which was kind of true. Kind of still is, come to think of it.

Jane was raised in the North Carolina mountains, and for years, she insisted "Bill" had two syllables and was pronounced "Bee-yull." She grew up in a household that experienced many financial hardships, which affected her deeply.

Jane's mom died of complications from early-onset Alzheimer's disease at age 62. Her dad, a good man if not always a fiscally wise one, took care of her mom until the day she died. For years, his financial decisions had given Jane cause to resent him. Yet the way he stepped up, and for years took care of his ailing wife, all but erased Jane's bitterness toward him.

But it didn't erase the wounds.

In 1992, the one wounded from the effects of poverty and the one wounded from the effects of abandonment, both said I do and became one flesh. Years of wondering if a true and lasting connection was even possible for someone like me were erased with her "I do," and then even more so with every passing year.

She says I was still rolling my head to go to sleep when we got married. Ugh. I thought I had stopped that sometime around college.

Jane got a good man. To minimize that would be to sell short the redemptive work that God had done in me. My heart of stone, as God aptly called it, has been exchanged with a heart of flesh that is the dwelling place of Christ.

But I'm going to rat myself out a little and tell you what this good man also brought to the marriage. She got a man who has serious touching issues, as in I don't like being touched. Taking the tiniest bit of liberty, I assume almost every woman wants, and needs, a man who will hold her at night, cuddle with her, offer sexless physical intimacy and closeness. It seems to be built into their DNA. Men, by and large, aren't wired that way. But from what I can tell, most men enjoy it at least a little, and at the very least, do it because it makes their wife happy.

I believe the Greek words to describe my actions in this category are Suckimus Maximus. In the Greek dictionary, Suckimus Maximus is defined as: Achieving a high level of suckitude, surpassed only by certain mythical creatures, the Ford Pinto (my first car, by the way) and tuna fish casserole with asparagus (a staple in my house growing up.)

I honestly believe that the smothering attention I got from Nana played no small role in me being so adverse to hugging, cuddling and most all things involving physical closeness. But even if that is 100 percent true, Jane has paid an unfair price that she didn't owe. And she's stayed.

I'd love to say that my aversion to cuddling sums up all of the ways in which Jane got the short end of the stick. But I've come this far with the vulnerability card, why stop now? I make weird noises for no reason at all sometimes, almost Tourette-like. I snore like a jackhammer, though that's a somewhat recent development. I don't do the household finances; I have zero mechanical or carpentry skills and easily get bored.

None of that would be good fodder for a dating website, so it's a good thing Jane is a stayer and loves me despite my somewhat unimpressive resume of husbanding.

I remember a few times, particularly during my panic attacks following 9/11, where I very much needed to be held securely by Jane, who never dreamed of withholding that, or even years later, bring it up as evidence that people do have those needs.

I never have felt worse than I did during those dark two months. Two or three panic attacks, two trips to the emergency room, uncontrollable crying, and I'm a guy who was never a crier. I had periods where my body felt numb or tingly from head to toe, and a brief couple of weeks or so when I had a hard time being out in public.

It further prepared me for what Rachel was about to go through. Of course, I didn't know that then.

Several times during those months, while I was sobbing in her arms, I would ask her if she was going to abandon me.

"No," she said. "I'll never leave you. You're stuck with me forever. You hear me? Forever."

What I needed from her, other than the assurance that she, too, was a stayer, was for her to take care the logistics of Rachel's medicines and appointments, talk to the school, keep up with the trivial parts of this unraveling mess while I took on the heavy emotional toll of being Rachel's rock.

I never said it that way. And its arrogant of me to think that God couldn't have just as easily chose and equipped Jane to take on this task. Often, I wish He had. But Jane had her own burdens to bear. One of them was me, because while I was committed to staying, I didn't have the emotional endurance or strength to take care of Rachel and me.

She took care of me. And mostly took care of Laura.

Even now, I can see that Jane is all of the things that I am not. She's organized. She's detailed. She's persistent and she's a hard worker. I am a hard worker some of the time. She is all of the time.

She recently turned 50 and I put together a "50 Shades of Jane" book. It was a compilation of birthday notes from friends and family going back as far as I could find. What others were saying about my wife reminded me how lucky I am.

"You are a beautiful queen," Laura wrote.

"You have fought countless battles for your family," Rachel wrote.

"Mom would be so proud of you," wrote her sister, Julie.

Friends used words for Jane such as "blonde-haired hotty, a trusted friend, compassionate, the friend I called, mentor and I see Jesus in her eyes."

She's type-A. I'm not. She loves lists; I don't. She is a rock star at work; I no longer am.

But we've got that one thing in common. Neither of us is going anywhere.

God said:

I was there, holding Jane while she was holding you. I'd later be holding you while you were holding Rachel. That's how this thing works, ya know? The battles you face are not against flesh and blood, but against spirits. There are some things in life that only I can fix for you. But you aren't made to go it alone. You need people to fight for your heart and stand beside you. Jane is No. 1 on that list.

Chapter 13 – Little Bill

"You will be called by a new name that the mouth of the Lord will bestow. You will be a crown of splendor in the Lord's hand." – Isaiah 62:2-3

"You are much closer to Little Bill than anything else. You want to be something more, like a masculine warrior. Please. Read your own book! You are vulnerable, and in all the wrong ways."
– The Deceiver.

Getting named the Great Stayer by God might well have saved me and my family. But it wasn't the first name I'd been given.

At birth, my parents gave me a name: William Arthurs Sanders, Jr. They threatened to call me Sandy, then settled on Bill. Eventually, in certain family circles, I'd be Little Bill and my dad was Big Bill.

Being Little Bill was fine for the most part. It seemed a necessary way to distinguish between the two of us when mom or Nana or a neighbor was hollering.

"Bill, phone's for you," mom would holler from downstairs.

"Which Bill?"

"Little Bill."

Stuff like that.

I was less OK with it after puberty. I'd answer the phone, in the days before caller ID, and a voice on the other end would ask to speak to Bill.

"Big Bill or Little Bill?" I'd ask. Usually I'd get a chuckle, then, "Big Bill." And for a split second, I'd feel emotionally small, embarrassed not that others might still call me Little Bill, but that I had just referred to myself as Little Bill.

In middle school, just as puberty was beginning to do its thing, peers give you a new name. And while we're not often called by those names, they become a weighty burden we wear around our neck. Star Quarterback? Sounds great, but it imagine the pressure of living up to it. Homecoming Queen? What girl wouldn't want that one? Maybe the one who's convinced she has nothing to offer except her good looks.

Queer. Slut. Mama's Boy. Nothing good about those.

By high school, the name becomes even more of an assigned label: The One Who Gets the Girls. The One Who Will Sleep With A Boy On The First Date. The One From the Trailer Park.

I was assigned a few names growing up. Nana named me "The One Who Needed To Be Babied." Charlotte named me "The One Not Worth Sticking Around For." That's how the two early significant women in my life saw me. It was emasculating, embarrassing and the opposite of what I wanted to be true about me. I wanted to be able the one who would stand up for himself and others and the one who was worth sticking around for.

Others gave me their names, too. And none of them were great.

It wasn't until I was 38 years old that God named me, and in doing so, told me how He saw me.

Like always, He didn't speak to me audibly. And like most of the time, I had to questions what he was telling me. But that night, while I was lying on Rachel's floor seeking some hope to cling to, He said to me: "You are the Great Stayer. He then assured me that I had heard him right. This was my name, how He saw me, my truest characteristic.

The Great Stayer, huh? I can think of about 100 adjective/noun combos that would be sexier, more adventurous and more heroic sounding than the Great Stayer. I can think of a few that sound as boring. But it's the one God was bestowing on me.

At a time of my life when the emotional pain of watching Rachel tremble, cower and physically hurt from fear, was draining me so dry, I get this.

I wasn't even asking for a name from Him. I was asking for one thing – that Rachel get better.

The Great Stayer, huh? The Great Milquetoast seems to be on the same page. Maybe The Great Do-Nothinger. At first blush, Great and Stay seemed to be on opposite ends of the spectrum. Doesn't great usually imply going, doing, conquering?

The first definition I found only solidified my initial impression: "To stop going forward." Perfect. I'm The Great Stopper of Going Forward."

Next definition: "To stop doing something, to continue in place or condition."

Anyone want to fight me for this moniker yet?

Then: "To stand firm."

OK. That has an appeal, I guess.

Then I struck gold: "To stick or remain with, as in a race, or a trial of endurance. To remain the whole time. To fix on something as a foundation. To provide physical or moral support, as in, to sustain."

Really, God? You think I am great at that?

If this was sewn into my DNA as God was claiming, it was certainly something I would have to mature into, because staying didn't come naturally to me. I'm prone to wander; Lord I feel it. But then, I'm not sure staying comes naturally for anyone. Staying meant seeing things I didn't want to see. It meant hurting when others hurt. Not leaving or pretending that the bad wasn't happening.

I remembered how growing up, I could not stay to watch an after-school playground fight. Other boys would flock to it and jockey for position; I'd flee. I wished I wanted to be there. I wanted to have the stomach to watch one kid wrestle another one to the floor, get on top of him, and bloody his nose. Why couldn't I like it? Was that really too much to ask? I was fine right up to the moments when the first punch was thrown. Then I'd feel this bizarre concoction of emotions – sadness and anger and almost a physical sickness, like I was the one taking a gut punch.

But what I felt was more about me than it was about the kid getting punched. The bigger feeling was shame, and it would set up residence within me. Once the schoolyard fight started, I would leave. I couldn't bear to feel someone else's pain. It was empathy, and a spiritual gift of compassion and encouragement. But it was also fear and I couldn't find the courage to stand up for the victim, or if needed, for myself.

So I left.

Being empathetic and compassionate would be great for a father and husband. But they were lousy things for a kid trying to make his way though suburban middle and high school.

I went through those years trying to stay away from scenes that would cause my heart to hurt for someone else. I turned my back when I could and I pretended it wasn't happening.

I began working out a lot. In high school I took weight-training courses whenever I could. I was a slightly taller-than-average kid, with a nice-enough build. I could lift more weight than most people in my weight-training classes. And the bench press my specialty. I had a big chest and decent-sized arms. At 15 years old, weighing about 155, I could bench 225 pounds. Pound for pound, there was not a stronger kid than me in the class.

But I couldn't find where to sign up for the shame-training course. The outward muscles were just that – on the outside, not a part of the real me. How was I so intimidated and bullied at a time that I clearly had the strength to take care of myself against 99 percent of the boys?

I had no mean streak, which again would become good as an adult, but it didn't help a 15-year-old trying to prove he had what it took to be a man.

There was a TV show I watched as a kid that had me pegged – *Happy Days*. I was the kind, easy going, if somewhat gullible Richie Cunningham, desperately wanting to be the much cooler Fonzie. Actually, Richie had some moments of reluctantly standing up to his bullies. In one episode in which Richie was being picked on and ordered to mimic the "bings and bongs" of a malfunctioning pinball machine, The Fonz convinced Richie that he had what it took to stand up to them.

It was in how he clenched his teeth, squinted his eyes and talked using a deep voice and the right words. Richie believed him because, well, he was The Fonz. Richie confronted his bully, who of course didn't back down from Richie's ridiculous attempt to look and sound like someone he wasn't – a tough kid.

The Fonz pulled him aside and confessed that the he had forgotten one key piece of this puzzle. You had to have actually hit a guy before; you had to have at least the base of a reputation that you could and would, back up the tough talk if needed.

I learned the talk and the look, and I had the muscles. But I lacked the reputation.

Maybe I am more Ralph Malph, the likeable kid who no one took seriously, a kid who fit in with many different groups of kids, but was always on the periphery, expendable, frequently left out, usually welcomed but almost never invited.

The first time I realized my pecking order in the social scene was a few years earlier, in the fifth grade. We were still living in Orlando and had a pool in our backyard, which wasn't a big deal in Orlando, but it still was better than not having one. I was turning 10 years old and had invited my basketball team over for a birthday pool party. I played it somewhat cool, not sending out childish invitations, but just making sure the guys knew about it. My dad was going to grill burgers and we'd do the most audacious diving board stunts we could come up with. It would be great.

Patrick, my nine-year-old buddy from up the street was the

first to arrive. Fine, whatever. He isn't on the team and is the least-anticipated guest to my party. But he brought a present of some sort, so fine, I'll hang with him until the important guys arrive. But then he'll be on his own to blend in for a while before hopping on his bike and riding back to his house.

But no one else came.

The truth is, I didn't really care about the party, and those kids were not particularly close to me. But it was still a crushing moment, an introduction, or re-introduction, to embarrassing shame and vulnerability.

The lesson I learn that day: Do not leave my heart exposed again. Do not risk that I will be accepted, loved or even liked.

And for goodness sakes, never, ever have another birthday party.

And until I was 30 years old and had no say in the matter because it was a surprise, I didn't.

****

So now, at 38, God is telling me I'm The Great Stayer. And now, to me, staying means all of the above things. It has meant staying in the arena of my kids' lives. It has meant staying with Jane, through thick and thin. It's meant staying in the battle for the hearts of friends when cancer take their spouse, or when divorce comes to my best friend 28 years into his marriage, or when a friend's teenage daughter dies out of the blue. It meant not checking out emotionally or mentally.

To be great at those things? Really God? What a great, name.

I assumed God had given me this name because I had earned it. How wrong I was. He had given me the name in advance of sending into the heat of this battle, the one that Little Bill couldn't fight.

God said:

First, c'mon. As if I would give you a new name and have it be a lame one. And I gave you a pretty awesome role model to learn about the name I'd give you decades later. The stakes for him staying were huge. For you, for Cindy. For Rachel.

As for the pool party, I know a thing or two about rejection too. And I know how it feels. I won't for a second minimize the effect that had on your life.

And so you weren't The Fonz? You do know The Fonz wasn't really The Fonz, either, right?

But you are The Great Stayer. And you won't cower from this fight. You'll face it and fight it head on, heroically.

Chapter 14 – Hello Rachel

"For I know the plans I have for you, declares the Lord, plans for welfare and not for evil, to give you a future and a hope." – Jeremiah 29:11

"These are going to be my favorite years. You'll see just how little your efforts matter."
– The Deceiver

In 1993, Rachel was born, two days after my first wedding anniversary. I remember going home that night, while Jane and Rachel were still in the hospital, and lying down in my bed. No one had ever been as overwhelmed as me in that moment, not Geronimo, not Butch Cassidy, not Walter Mondale the night before he lost 525-13 to Ronald Reagan in 1984.

Do I have what it takes to do this? Of course, I don't. But I've still got 18 hours or so before they get home, maybe I can figure it out between now and then.

I was years from putting the two and two together of God saying: *"Yeah Bill, you have what it takes. Remember what it feels like to be abandoned? Rachel will never have a clue of what that feels like. You, my child, are The Great Stayer. You will stay in the arena and in the many fights life will bring."*

I was not ever known as The Great Anything, until except the stayer name. And I guess it probably is what I have done best for the past 23 years of marriage and fatherhood.

I never really thought I could go out on my own and do better than what I had at home, which made staying easier. I have a hot wife who loves to cook and loves to love me, and I've got two daughters – Laura was born in 1996 – who have 10 fingers and 10 toes and have the capacity to show tremendous love.

For me, the appeal of not staying had nothing to do with getting away from the madness of parenthood. (OK, maybe a little. My house, at times was a three-ring circus.) But mostly, it was the appeal of giving my heart a rest, permission to not feel, to not worry and to not feel the intense weight of responsibility.

I'm sure on some level that's every man's thought pattern. For some, it probably includes the more obvious lures of something more tangible or sexier. For me, it was simply permission to be off duty. I was convinced Rachel was going to need every morsel of fierce relentlessness I could muster. And it was going to have to be served with a tenderhearted, patient and empathetic spirit, day after day, night after night.

Are you sure, God, that I can do this?

Along with Jane, I was raising a little Bill, named Rachel. Me, a little wounded, fragile kid full of fears, grew up and begat a little, wounded, fragile kid full of fears. The apple didn't fall far.

Rachel would not experience any trauma even close to what I did. But her anxiety disorder was stronger than mine ever was.

Almost immediately after bringing her home, certainly by the time she had her first episode of anxiety, I assumed Rachel required all of my heart, all of the time. Isn't that what the best father's do, commit their whole heart to their kids?

On top of that, I tried to add to the equation and offer all my solutions, all my deal-making with God and all my worrying.

Everything but offering my heart while simultaneously surrendering her wellbeing to Him, was wasted effort. It simply wore me out and left me more and more frustrated. My solutions, my deal making, my worrying ALWAYS amounted to bupkis.

So obviously, I quit worrying, quit trying to fix things, and stopped trying to swing deals with God. That would have been what The Great Learner would have done or The Great Faith Man. I was only The Great Stayer, remember?

So I'd fall back to my default mode equation: Wholeheartedness, plus problem solving, plus deal making, plus worrying equals the way to parent/treat/love/fix Rachel. And I was convinced being convinced she needed all those to be parented, treated, loved, and even fixed.

But Rachel didn't need fixing. She needed more than that. She needed emotional, physical and mental healing. I didn't have the ability to do that for myself, much less for someone else.

Fortunately, healing is what God offers. Frustratingly, it only comes in His perfect timing, which rarely fits our imperfect perception of timing. It certainly wasn't fitting mine.

God was offering that emotional protection to me, too, even though I hadn't yet realized I needed it. He was preventing my good and tender heart from going to unrecoverable places while I waffled on offering Rachel to Him and his timing, then grabbed her back because I didn't trust Him, then offered her back when I realize whether I trusted him or not, He, the author of this tale of rescue and redemption, was our only hope.

Rachel had begun having night terrors at the age of 2. Most every parent has heard the term. Most think they've experienced it. Most are kidding themselves. A night terror usually occurs about two or three hours after the child goes to sleep. Screaming ensues: Imagine what you think a kid would do if her appendix burst or if her shoulder slipped out of socket, or if a demon had possessed her. That's the kind of crying it was. It was like a horror movie. She was the kid you'd see who would be stiff as a board and have a glazed, icy stare and nothing would snap her out of it. None of the surefire diversions or tricks would ease the terror.

I do not know a parent who has truly gone through these in which the first one didn't include a car ride to the emergency room. The first one is that startling and unsettling. The next dozen or so, we had it better than some, were not as startling. But to me, they were every bit as unsettling.

Every night, I'd go to bed worried that tonight was gonna be the night. I had long since quit rolling my head, thank you Jesus, but praying a ritualistic prayer every night still seemed fine. "Please don't let Rachel have a night terror tonight, Jesus."

For a while, I went to bed expecting Him to answer my prayer favorably, to smile on our night and on our Rachel. But on so many nights, around 1:30 a.m. or so, I'd be awakened by Rachel's terror. The next night I'd pray the same prayer. And the next. And every time Rachel would have a night terror, my faith that God cared about my prayers took a little hit.

I have never heard God or Jesus audibly, but a couple of years into the terrors and the prayers, while lying in bed, I got the most definitive word from God I had ever gotten, and I remember it vividly.

"These night terrors are going to happen again. But the end is near. Hang on."

True enough, it happened again. But not for much longer. On the night of her fourth birthday, maybe a few months after that promise, Rachel had her last night terror.

And as terror-less nights began to add up, God's promise became something for me to hang onto, to put in my back pocket and pull out when my faith would become weak. And I'd need it in spades. Because while there were no more night terrors after Rachel's fourth birthday, her anxiety was just getting started. And my faith would be challenged to its core.

When she was seven, Rachel was diagnosed with ADHD. Her teachers had seen it in her even at such a young age. And Jane suspected it too. I figured it out when I took her to an Atlanta Braves baseball game. From the time we got into the car until we got out some six hours later, she did not stop talking. I had never seen anything like it. Six billion questions and the majority of them were about nothing. It wore me out. I know every kid goes through this phase, but Rachel, at least that night, was a world-class talker on steroids.

"Where are we going to park?"

"How much money do you think that man has?"

"How many cars are on the road, right now?"

My answer to most questions that night was: "I don't know."

Her next statement was always the same: "Guess."

"I have no idea, Sweetie,"

"But if you had to guess?"

"Ten thousand."

"Why not a million?"

It was relentless.

I had no idea what she was doing. Neither did she. The constant need to talk, and to be heard, was her connecting with someone else, and staying connected. Connection was the only tool Rachel had in young, undeveloped bag of tricks to fight her fears.

When I got home that night, after briefly filling in Jane about our night, I sat down on the couch, by myself in a quiet room and had two thoughts: First, her teachers were probably right. Second, loving Rachel wildly was great but it was not going to be enough. Still, I was going to have to learn how to embrace the unique level of energy that Rachel brought to the almost every setting. If I miss out on loving what makes Rachel who she is, then I'm going to end up exhausted and totally frustrated, and fail her. If I embrace it, I'll still end up being exhausted, and at least occasionally frustrated. But I also think I'll have a lifelong invitation to stay in her life's arena, and a chance to be her hero. What dad doesn't want that?

And soon enough, she'll need a hero.

And, as for me? Well, I've been needing the chance to be a hero since those days of having my books knocked out of my hands.

****

In 2002, I saw a therapist for the first time – if you don't count the vertigo session, which I don't, because it was purely procedural. My breaking point started on 9/11 and had culminated over a week in February 2002, where I flat out could not function.

The events of 9/11 were enough to send anyone into a mode of panic and anxiety. But I'm certain, for me, it was the final straw on a heap that had been weighing me down for some time.

I woke up not feeling well that morning and was moving slowly. I'd felt a little flu-ish for a couple of days, but not bad enough to miss work. Right as I was about to leave the house, I saw reports of the first plane hitting the World Trade Center. I lived about 45 minutes from the AJC and listened to the news the whole way in.

I had gotten to the newsroom in time to see the second plane hit the tower.

There was no preparing for this kind of event, but like most around me that day, I was good with deadlines and breaking news, having worked and excelled in covering some horrific and dangerous stories.

I was fine for most of the day. But by about 5 p.m., I was not. I felt dizzy, lightheaded, like I was walking on a trampoline instead of a cement floor. My day should have been about halfway over. But I couldn't stay.

I drove home, went to bed and then had a full-fledged panic attack. My heart raced, my breathing was labored and I had this tingly numbness from head to toe. I'd never heard of such symptoms, much less thought about having them myself.

Neither had Jane.

She took me to E.R. I had not had a heart attack, the doctors assured Jane. It was a panic attack, treated with an anti-anxiety drip and a prescription to fill the next day.

I was not right, though, for several months. I had a couple other panic attacks, and after the second one, at least I knew what it was, and that it wasn't going to kill me. But it was a dark, scary few months nonetheless.

Then one day, I started crying. And I couldn't stop. For about a week, in early February, I cried a dozen times a day and didn't feel like leaving the house. I assumed I was going crazy.

I wasn't.

But I was getting a taste of what Rachel's life was going to be like for the next few years. I'm certain my empathy and understanding of her debilitating anxiety would have been significantly less had I not experienced it firsthand.

Anxiety is often a sister of depression. But I was not depressed, neither clinically nor practically. I had been a nervous child and nervous adolescent and now I was a nervous father. Bottled up for years, the tension was bound to erupt. And it did.

Shortly after I began coming out of my fog, Rachel entered the depths of hers.

Rachel had her first panic attack on the school bus one afternoon in the fall of seventh grade. She got nervous because she felt trapped. And as a 12 year old on a school bus, she was trapped. She began hyperventilating, something she'd never heard of, much less experienced. The seemingly unstoppable rapid breathing made her arms and legs began to tingle, then to feel like she was being stuck by a million little pins, then go numb altogether. Her heartbeat was racing, she got dizzy and she thought she was going to die.

The bus pulled over, Rachel got out and laid on the sidewalk as her friend Caroline, and the bus driver, tried to comfort her.

"We'll call you an ambulance, sweetie," the bus driver said.

That made it worse. Rachel, rightfully so, equated ambulances with something really, really bad.

Jane and I were both downtown at work. Caroline called her dad, who raced over to pick Rachel up while a bus full of kids waited.

Caroline's dad called Jane and described what was going on. We both knew exactly what it was. She was having a panic attack. What we didn't know was what this was signaling. By the time Jane got home, Rachel was resting at Caroline's house, the panic having subsided. For now.

God said:

There's nothing worse than hurting for your child. I know. Just like during the hard years of your childhood, sugarcoating it, pretending it wasn't as bad as it was, I won't do that. I summoned the angels on so many occasions to intervene and to protect you and Rachel. There was a war, a real, raging battle that was being fought on behalf of Rachel and you on spiritual planes.

Chapter 15 – Middle School

"Be anxious for nothing, but in everything by prayer and supplication, with thanksgiving, let your requests be made known to God; and the peace of God, which surpasses all understanding, will guard your hearts and minds through Christ Jesus." – Philippians 4:6-7

"He's holding out on you, ya know?"
– The Deceiver

From the time Rachel turned four and quit having night terrors to the day of her first panic attack, we'd seen her anxiety build little by little. She stopped being willing to sleep over at friends' houses. She started acting afraid at night and wanted assurances that we'd stay awake until she went to sleep, not matter how long that took. She wanted our door to be open, or if not open, then cracked where she could see that the lights were still on. Of course, all that made sense to me. I'd lived that same childhood.

She had begun to feel less comfortable in some of her classes, less sure of herself, more sure that something wasn't right in her body or in her head.

We started taking her to child psychiatrists and counselors. When the counseling yielded no results, they began to introduce medicines that felt certain would do the trick.

So the panic attack didn't catch us totally off guard.

"We'll take you to school tomorrow and one of us will pick you up," Jane said. "You don't have to ride the bus tomorrow, or the rest of week."

Her next panic attack was only a few days later, in school. The symptoms were the same – loss of control, a feeling of being constricted, out-of-control breathing, racing heartbeats – a sense that she was about to pass out or die.

By time I got from downtown to her school to pick her up, she looked gaunt, frail and largely absent. Physically, she looked nothing like she had two weeks ago. I'm sure she hadn't lost weight, and I guess she was always a little on the pale side. But what I saw that afternoon, and would see hundreds of times more over the next few years, was a lifeless, hopeless look of a dying kid, a skeleton of a life.

Pretty soon, this was her normal. If she didn't have full-fledged panic attacks every day, she didn't have a single day that any kid would call good.

Jane and I had to arrange our work schedules so somebody was always home. We'd drive her to school, pray with her and watch her get all the way into the school before we'd drive off.

Almost without fail, within an hour or two of us taking her to school, she was calling from the clinic's office.

On my days at home, I'd try to get a little work done, but really what I was doing was waiting for the phone to ring. I'd shower with the phone on the other side of the shower glass so I could not only hear it ring, but I could see who was calling.

Every morning was the same. "Please God, let today be the day the phone doesn't ring. Please let her be able to…"

And the phone rang.

The caller ID says its Durham Middle School calling. Caller ID has never been as unnecessary as it was during those months. When the phone rang during school hours, and it wasn't Durham, I was surprised. I would briefly be relieved when I saw it was Jane calling, or even a telemarketer. No one had ever loved getting a call from a telemarketer like I did during this period. But then, a few minutes later, it would ring again. This time, it would be Durham.

Most of the time, it was Rachel, not the nurse, on the other end. When she was having a particularly bad panic attack, the nurse would call, but the garden-variety anxiety attack meant Rachel would call. Her voice was weak, frail, timid and full of shame. Every single time, it was the same.

"Hey," she'd say, in that voice that I've never heard from her except on those calls.

"Hey, Sweetie."

"I have anxiety."

"You know I'm only 10 minutes away. Do you think you can take your medicine and stay in the clinic for a few minutes, then go back to class?"

"I'll try."

"Call me if you can't. I'll come get you."

We'd long since learned that encouraging her to relax or calm down or telling her to think through this rationally was like telling a kid with a bad stomach flu to suck it up and go eat some lunch.

Twenty minutes later, maybe an hour, she'd call back, and I'd go pick her up. Seventh grade is just about every girl's most awkward age. Rachel was tallish and thin and had big eyes and two big front teeth that competed for dominance on her face. When I'd pick her up, she just looked sick. I say this with the utmost respect for parents who have gone through cancer, but that's how Rachel looked when I'd pick her up from school, like a cancer patient, fresh off yet another chemo treatment, dying a little every day. And I was right there with her, dying a little every time the phone rang, too.

By the time she was 12, she had been prescribed practically

every antidepressant a pharmaceutical company had ever made, and many trial-and-error cocktail combinations of new drugs and old ones that were rarely prescribed anymore.

Other than ADHD drugs, Zoloft was the first drug doctors tried. This was a few years before the first panic attack, but a couple of years after we'd started to notice the anxieties building. Zoloft isn't recommended for 9 year olds. For good reason.

She'd eventually be prescribed Prozac, Wellbutrin, Cymbalta, imipramine, Buspar, Seroquel, Inderal, Adderall, Ritalin and Vistaril. And that's off the top of my head. Most of those aren't recommended for kids either. For good reason.

Often, a new medicine or combination would work for a few months and give us a little hope. But then her tolerance to it would increase and her fears would take back over, and we'd all be left exhausted and discouraged again.

We had to withdraw Rachel from school for the second semester of seventh grade and homeschool her. But it wasn't just school. Soon she became a complete shut-in, unable to risk going out anywhere in public. And then there were the nights.

There were months, probably at about 18 of them, where I had to lie down on her floor before she'd fall asleep. I'd sneak out quietly and catch a little TV before I crashed in my own bed. I knew I had maybe two hours to sleep before I'd be switching beds with her.

One night, before I even laid down on her floor, she was sitting in her bed and began to tear up.

"Daddy," she said, "I'm sorry, but I hate night so bad. Every day, I dread nighttime."

"What are you afraid of, sweetie?"

For a while it was that the house would burn. Then it was intruders. Then it was her natural mortality.

She knew how crazy this sounded, but she became superstitiously ritualistic with her good night question: "Promise I won't die tonight, and that nothing bad will happen to me tonight or tomorrow?"

Those were the exact words, recited, night after night, for more than a year. I said yes, every time, that I promised.

It was a little like that lie Cindy told me 30 years before this. But eventually, I took this question to God.

"Father," I asked, "Can I promise Rachel every night for the foreseeable future that she wouldn't die before she wakes, that nothing bad would happen to her that night or the next day?"

God said:

You may. I know the pain, the oppression, the fatigue in your house and in your family. As long as Rachel doesn't consider a bad grade or an insult or even run-of-the-mill fears that we're working on as 'bad', if her idea of bad is catastrophic, and for Rachel I know it always is right now, then yeah, make that promise. I'll make good on it. And my son, just like the night terrors when she was 2 and 3, we're not through the valley just yet. But we're getting there. We are going through it – which means into it and out of it. And we're gonna do it together. You've got my word on it."

God's "word on it" was great at first. But it became less and less great the longer this went on.

Remember, Rachel was depending on me to be her rock, to be the one who always understood, could always say the right thing, would never get frustrated by the disorder and could always usher her back into a sense that things were going to be OK.

I was game for the assignment. But I was woefully unable to be or do all of those things all of the time. And I began resenting God for seemingly placing such an arduous task on me.

I fasted a day a week for a while and prayed for Rachel upstairs while Jane. Rachel and Laura were eating downstairs.

I doubled-down on my Bible reading and quiet times, making sure I was doing my part to keep God happy with me, which in effect, would make Him smile on Rachel.

I was loving God and trusting Jesus the best I could.

But He wasn't coming through. Not for Rachel and not for me.

I was being abandoned. Again.

I never quit believing that He could change my situation and heal Rachel from her anxiety. That just made it worse. He could heal her, but He wasn't.

I'd heard in church somewhere that the ticket was to pray God's word back to him. So I did that.

"You say, Father, Fear not. That we were not given a spirit of fear, that you would have us be anxious for nothing. I claim that truth on behalf of my little girl, God."

I even rationalized to God why He had to heal her and not other sick children. After all, Jesus never called us not to have cancer or be in a tragic car crash. He did call us not to live in fear and anxiety.

I've prayed plenty of times in my life and not gotten the answer I think I deserved. None of them made me question whether prayer was essential and vital and worthwhile.

This did. It left me wondering if everything was so preordained that me petitioning God was a waste of my breath?

Then it got darker.

Praying for Rachel this way, using scripture and praying for what seemingly had to be in his will, and getting nothing? That was worse than abandonment. It was betrayal.

Not only did I not understand this monster called anxiety, not in my life and certainly not in Rachel's, but I didn't understand why God would give me this new name and then make it impossible to live up to. I couldn't reconcile how God could be OK with what was going on with one of his beloved little children.

From the first night terror, through the ensuing years of crippling anxiety, I little by little became obsessed with taking care of Rachel because, little by little, I was losing faith that I could trust God to take care of her. My assessment of how much the real God loved me was based on how well Rachel was responding to medicine.

And she wasn't responding very much at all.

I talked to other people of faith, depending on them to have enough faith for me, and tried to believe that God wasn't betraying us.

So I came to another conclusion: I was not praying the right words, or praying them often enough. I didn't have enough faith and I had better figure out a way to have more faith and love Him more if He was going to intervene.

I thought I knew better than to believe that self-effort theology, but I found myself buying into any version of the gospel that would help me get my girl fixed.

But there were no magic words. All of the acting like Super Christian with super chutzpah just wore me out more and did nothing to help Rachel.

By then, it was all about Rachel. Not only had I attempted to supplant God in the role of taking care of Rachel, her wellbeing and happiness was becoming my god. And that god sucked.

But even as I resented the burden, I couldn't let go of it. Rachel's anxiety had so absorbed me that it wasn't a something I could loosen my grip on let go of. I had held onto it so tightly, it was if her anxiety had been welded into my grip, essentially becoming an appendage.

And somehow, in the midst of this, I had convinced myself that I was not an enabler. Oh, I'd fess up to the fact that I was close to being one. But I was doing what had to be done, and love covers a multitude of sins and enablers aren't good people and I am.

So much truth and so much falsity in those statements. I was and am a good man. Love does cover a multitude of sin. I was doing what *I thought* had to be done. But I was enabling.

Hello. My name is Bill Sanders and I'm a recovering enabler.

Deep down, I felt I faced only two options: Take care of Rachel, no matter the cost, or fail her. There was no middle ground. And failing her was not an option. After what I'd experienced when a parent was heroic and what I'd seen what happened when one chose a selfish, cowardly and easy path, I would soldier on. Period. No matter the cost.

I would be a stayer even if God was not going to be.

How had I gotten to a place where I needed God to save me from myself and save Rachel from my own madness?

****

During this time, we had to be in eyesight of her at all times. And by we, it was preferably, me. I remember a Christmas party our neighbors threw. The Rodgers lived directly behind us. At that time of year, with the leaves off the trees, Rachel, 12, could look out our den window and into the back porch and kitchen area of the Rodgers' house. Laura was 9.

We took the seemingly ridiculous extra step of hiring a babysitter.

Jane and I were at the party for about 15 minutes when we got the call that Rachel was having a panic attack. Fifty yards and within clear eyesight was too far for her. Even with a trained babysitter who Rachel liked, and who knew of Rachel's issues.

I didn't care a thing about the party. The Rodgers are fine people, but I was probably ready to leave anyway. But I wasn't ready for Rachel to need me to leave. It was one of the worst nights of my life because it showed me how unrealistic and ridiculously short my leash on freedom was and how helpless and hopeless things had become for Rachel. It was rock bottom.

But here's what I learned about rock bottom. There is some relief in knowing, or at least believing, that there was no deeper darkness to spiral into. I was as there in the heart of the cave of despair, and I was still alive. So was Rachel.

It was a glimmer of good and hope. And I do mean a glimmer, one that I had to re-embrace a level of faith to even call it a glimmer.

"He has sent me to bind up the brokenhearted, to proclaim freedom for the captives and release from darkness for the prisoners." – Isaiah 61:1

The night of the Rodgers' party became a night I could remind her of – not to shame her, but to encourage her, to remind her how far she'd come once she began on the slow and bumpy road to emotional health. It was easy for Rachel, and for us, to get discouraged when we seemingly took one of the hundreds of U-turns on that road to recovery.

But then God would remind me of that night. And I would remind Rachel. And we'd agree that wherever we were, we were ahead of where we were that night.

God said:

Not a single prayer went unheard. Not a single tear was cried in your house that I didn't match, tenfold. You doubted my faithfulness. I understand. But I stayed faithful. I promise. You doubted that I loved you and Rachel in a real way. I get that, too. But I loved you and Rachel with a love that is beyond comprehension and I still do. And guess what? If and when you doubt me again, I'll still be here. Nothing will change on my end. I'll keep hold of you and Rachel and Jane and Laura. I'm the one with the trustworthy grip here. So relax in that truth.

Chapter 16 – The Good Shrink

"I gain understanding from your precepts;
therefore I hate every wrong path."
– Psalms 119:104

"Go see another doctor. It won't help. There is no
helping this Rachel of yours" – The Deceiver

A s I said, from the time Rachel was 9 to the time she was 16, we took her to every child psychologist and psychiatrist we could find. Some of them had no business tending to a child with severe anxiety disorder, acting as if taking the authoritative route, somehow, would be helpful.

"You *will* sit here in this room and listen as your mother and I discuss this," one therapist told Rachel, who felt trapped in a room that to her, felt bouncy, like it was suspended on cables. "No you **may not** go out in the hall."

I was in on many of the appointments; I wish I had been in on this one.

Other doctors would use the tried-and-true play therapy sessions to attempt to uncover whatever repressed horror inside of Rachel that needed to be brought to the surface. Soon enough, though, they would tire of Rachel. She was a handful, and she wasn't an easy fix.

Most doctors – OK, that's painting it too broadly, but many of the ones we saw – didn't like being unsuccessful with more than one or two approaches. Maybe with a kid who wasn't such a handful. But not with one who was.

When Rachel was 15, we took her to a psychiatrist in Nashville, Tennessee, four hours from our home, because his methods and approach matched that of a nationally renowned brain expert in California, Dr. Daniel Amen, whom we had been recently reading about. We didn't expect a miracle. We'd grown weary of expecting much of anything from the medical community, and at times, from God.

Dr. Robert Hunt is a bit of a hippie, with a laid-back approach to just about everything. He had a grey Weimaraner dog that unassumingly greeted visitors at door and set the tone that this wasn't your typical doctor's office. His place was actually an old house a block away from the art district. I don't think he used the word "groovy," but if he had, it wouldn't have sounded like an old fuddy-duddy trying too hard.

He was completely for real.

He visited with Rachel for maybe 20 or 30 minutes. Then he met with Jane and me. He told us how delightful our child was. We hadn't heard that from a doctor in some time. Then he looked at us squarely and said: "I can help her. I'm sure of it."

What? You really think you can help my little girl, the one dripping with anxiety, soaked in fear and jumpy as a solider with PTSD?

"Yep. I can. I've seen a few Rachels before. I've even seen worse. I got this."

That night, we stayed in the Gaylord Opryland Hotel. The hotel's huge glass atrium ceilings provided canopy to thousands of tropical plants, waterfalls, trails and trees. To us, it offered therapy, refuge, sanctuary and hint of what Eden was like. The beauty and tranquility transfixed Rachel. And that transfixed us.

We left Nashville the next day a different family. A very qualified, if quirky, doctor who knew a few things about emotional disorders told us Rachel's life was going to get better. We had seen a glimpse of what that could look like at the Gaylord Hotel. We'd start seeing them more often. By some standards, Rachel would be a complete mess for years to come. In our eyes, she was on the way to being healed.

We made two or three trips a year to see Dr. Hunt for a few years. Each time, we stayed at the Gaylord, and each time we found peace and rest and hope to fuel us for another six months.

There is no other family traveling experience that came close to the Gaylord for us. We are a bad traveling family. We all like our space and Rachel and Laura tend to fight like cats and dogs. Just not at the Gaylord.

The medicines Dr. Hunt prescribed were not the miracle. In fact, the trial-and-error phase continued for a while. And Dr. Hunt wasn't around Rachel enough to make a huge impact on her from a therapeutic perspective. And by no means was the road we would travel the next several years bump free. It was full of potholes and detours and roadblocks.

My friend, Don Boykin, taught me something that was critical in my ability to stay in this fight. His wife had been diagnosed with a cancer. She had a tumor about a centimeter from her spine. Surgery was necessary, but the risks were high. Doctors didn't know if they would be able to get the entire tumor. They didn't know if Lynn would come out of the surgery paralyzed. They *didn't* know way more than they *did* know.

Lynn came through the surgery. Doctors got all of the tumor, and she had no paralysis. There was much rejoicing on that hospital hall by the dozens of church friends who had come to pray over Lynn and then to celebrate the good news.

Amid the rejoicing, God spoke a somewhat odd word to Don: *"Don't judge My love for Lynn and for you by the blessings/miracles I do in your lives."*

What? Of course, this is an indication of just how much God loved Don and Lynn, right? They were missionaries. They were spiritual warriors. Surely Don had misheard what God was telling him.

"Don't judge how much I love you and Lynn by the blessings or miracles I do in your lives. My love for you and Lynn is not conditional."

Not tying God's love for me and for Rachel to the blessings he might or might not give? It sounded so right, so obvious to someone who'd been a believer for decades.

Fifteen years later, on January 24, 2012, Lynn died from complications of cancer and heart disease, brought on by the cancer treatments.

"God's love did not lessen for Lynn and me that day," Don said.

And the verse that I had fought with for years came to mind.

"Come to Me, all who are weary and heavy-laden, and I will give you rest. Take My yoke upon you and learn from Me, for I am gentle and humble in heart, and you will find rest for your soul. For My yoke is easy and My burden is light." (Matt. 11: 28-30, NIV)

I had fought this verse because I was a living contradiction to it.

It didn't fully sink in for a few more years, but the assignment to be all things at all times to Rachel was not from God. I had given that impossible job to myself, and then begrudgingly wondered why I was suffocating under the weight of a burden that was anything but light. It was never intended for me.

Realizing that didn't change a thing about how quickly Rachel got better. It had everything to do with how thoroughly I was healed..

God loved Rachel and me just as much during the horrible times as the great times. His love hadn't changed. He loved us in our metro Atlanta home. Why He chose to meet us – in ways we'll never forget – through a hippie doctor in Nashville? I have no idea. But He did. And it's in my back pocket now.

God said:

I love the tropical plants and the sound of waterfalls too. And Dr. Hunt? He is a bit eccentric, isn't he? I know I heard him say 'groovy' more than once. Just when you needed it the most, I sent you to someone who would smile on you, and on Rachel. We could have done it in Atlanta. But Dr. Hunt needed to meet you guys. He needed Rachel to smile on him. I know this has been so much more than was tough, Bill. I know that it drained you till there was nothing left in your tank. I'm so proud of you.

Chapter 17 –
The Softball Years

"A friend loves at all times, and a brother is born for adversity." – Proverbs 17:17

"Mike doesn't care for you or about you. Fool!"
– The Deceiver

R achel and I grew tighter on the softball fields.
She started playing at 9, at the beginning of her most anxious years. It wasn't a panacea, but she had more good days than bad early on as the field slowly became a sanctuary for her.

In all, she played for 10 years and became a very good player. At first, she was far from good – awkward and lacking grace, not to mention any care or attentiveness in her approach to the game. So in her second year, I figured she needed a coach who would look past the gawkiness and hyperactivity and give her a shot at playing and enjoying the game. That meant me, of course. I wanted her to stick with it. She needed a crack at staying with something. And a connection outside of our emotional dependence on each other was definitely in order.

Only trouble was, I didn't know how to coach softball. I'd never done it. It wasn't particularly difficult of course, and with 10-year-old girls, all I really needed was the Hippocratic oath of doing no harm. But soon, I'd morph that into a Hippocratic scale of practical justice: "Do as little harm as possible." I think I did that, but there might be varying opinions on that.

Regardless, coaching girls' softball became a gift from God, to Rachel and me. And it would challenge me to live up to my true name.

I can't say I knew it was a gift when I started in 2002, but it came with this simple operating instruction: *"Handle with care. For there are hundreds of little hearts you are about to impact. Some are hard and need softening. Some are broken and need healing. Some are lonely and need loving. Some have been abandoned. Some are desperate and need saving. And all need a stayer in their lives."*

In hindsight, the message made perfect sense – but only in hindsight.

"For every one of those little girls who really will need you, there will be five who won't. It'll be really hard to figure out

which ones need what – at first, anyway. But stay in it. And in the meantime, side on loving them all.

"For in this gift, you will be made known to hundreds of kids and their parents. Many, if not all, will judge you. That's okay. They will see Me in you. And even though you will be flawed and won't handle every moment with the grace that represents the true you, you are, and will be, blameless in My eyes."

A dozen years later, the message would be:

"You took this gift without knowing it was a gift. You were unsure of yourself and the assignment, but you allowed me to influence lives through you. You saw that, but you doubted it. I'm thrilled you no longer doubt it.

A couple years ago I asked that you offer it back to me and trust I knew what I was doing. You did. And I took care of you. I know that softball and these girls are that important to you. That's why you are doing it again. If I ask you to lay it down again, I know you will trust me again, and that I know what I'm doing."

So my prayer became: "Thank you for the gift. When it's time for me to move on in ministry, help me to give it back to you and not obsess over it and try to snatch it back from you. For I am prone to do such."

If it seems God and I have a lot of talks about softball, it's because we do. Why would we not? The fields are where my heart is most alive. He knew this about me long before I did. But it hasn't come without challenges.

****

In the fall of 2011, it looked like I was done with coaching softball, and even with a few significant relationships.

Even more has happened since. Predictably, God was faithful throughout. Equally predictably, I bounced back and forth from trusting, accepting and waiting to scheming, rationalizing and pouting. Was I really done with what I cared about so much?

Like He promised, He took care of it, and of me.

He proved He knew me. He knew that my trust would waver. But instead of punishing me or setting me up for more hurt, He did what He does best. He took my failure and made something beautiful of it.

Many things slowly got me to the place where He asked me to give the gift back. But what happened afterwards was the real story.

In her 11th year and roughly 25th team (having played fall, spring and sometimes summer teams), Rachel decided she wanted to play one more season. I had enough friends at the park that I was sure she'd get on a team she and I were comfortable with.

When I found out Mike Matthews was coaching a team, I figured that was perfect and we'd be playing with him and his daughter, Erin.

Unfortunately, he didn't pick Rachel.

As far as I was concerned, Mike was one of my best softball friends. Though we had not connected much outside of softball, within the West Cobb Association, we were tight. I had coached Erin a few times and I'd chosen him as an assistant coach when I had my first all-star team in 2007. At least once, I remembered Mike's traveling preventing him from coaching; he asked me to pick Erin in the draft. And of course, I did.

Erin was a good player and besides, that's what friends do. And now he had the chance to repay the kindness by choosing Rachel to be on his team. And in my mind, he failed us.

I was bewildered. That old feeling of betrayal and abandonment, my default setting, came back strongly.

It was particularly hurtful because, behind the scenes, I had been blackballed from having my own team by the league's board president somewhere around 2011. I say "somewhere around 2011" because there are times when more coaches sign up than are needed. Later I would find out that a couple of parents didn't like the amount of playing time their daughter got during all-stars. Even though every parent had to sign a contract before all-stars, acknowledging that along with other differences from rec ball, playing time wasn't guaranteed. It had to be earned and it was at the discretion of the head coach.

I played everyone in every tournament, which was more inclusive than some parents wanted. I didn't play every girl equally, which was less inclusive than others wanted. Typical ballpark politics, really.

Although I had coached the 25 teams, none of that mattered now. . Along the way, I'm sure I ruffled some feathers. I remember really screwing up at least one time. But it had never involved Erin or Mike.

The backstory of the royal screw up is this: In 2009, one of my pitchers that I'd coached once or twice before for some reason couldn't throw a strike this season. She was quiet, always did what was asked of her, and would do so smiling. Her dad was always around too. He was supportive, friendly, willing to help, but didn't meddle. They were great to have on a team.

But one night, we were down to eight girls, which meant only two players in the outfield. At their age, four outfielders were often not enough to get the job done. But our main pitcher was running late and our third baseman was missing as well. So I told Michelle she was pitching.

In the moment, I couldn't read her. Usually, I'm decent at that. And such things matter to me. But in this case, I had no idea whether she wanted to take the mound. She was poker facing it.

She had struggled mightily to pitch in a previous game. Walking batter after batter had to be embarrassing and I know it was frustrating for restless parents to watch as well. I had asked her dad after that game if she still wanted to pitch.

"She'll do whatever you need her to do," he said.

Love the attitude, but it was of no help.

So, with no other option on this night, I put her in to pitch. And when she struggled again, I took a page from the brilliant coaching guidebook and offered a nugget of coaching gold from the dugout.

After eight straight balls, all of them landing a foot in front of the plate, I encouragingly shouted, *"Put a little more on it!"*

The glance back from the pitcher said, "Thanks a lot Coach! I hadn't thought about that."

In short, it was less than helpful advice.

But Michelle was the only one there who had ever pitched. And I'm pretty sure she wanted to be pitching. I didn't want that for her though, and not because I wanted to win, which I always wanted to do, but because I couldn't stand watching her out there alone, struggling so badly.

After about five batters, Molly, my third-base player and number two pitcher, came running in from the parking lot.

Feeling a bit of relief, I called time out and quickly put Molly on the mound and told Michelle to go to third base. Molly struggled to throw strikes, too, and I knew for sure that she would rather be playing third base. But she was tough. I wasn't sure whether Michelle would be broken by walking batter after batter in front of parents and friends, but I knew Molly wouldn't be.

By now, eight batters had come to the plate, and seven of them had walked. So when I saw Haley running in, the one girl I knew could throw strikes, it seemed a no-brainer. She was my tenth player, so no substitution was necessary. I told her to get in there and pitch. She looked at me like, "Duh."

I sent Molly to third and Michelle to right field.

Now, no one likes right field except the girls who don't want to play much. But I wasn;t clearly thinking about that in the mad rush of getting two just-arrived girls onto the field. With Haley on the mound, the inning mercifully ended a few batters later.

Before Michelle could get to the dugout, her dad had come to the fence and told me that she was done. He said Michelle was going to get her softball bag and was leaving the park right then and there.

And she did. She never rejoined the team.

I had done nothing willfully wrong. And I hadn't had time to come up with a better solution. But willfully or not, I'd offended a dad and perhaps his little girl. And his reaction, while not ideal, was totally understandable.

I emailed him as soon as I got home and fell on the sword as hard as I could. I'd made a mistake, screwed up, and I apologized. I asked him to please tell Michelle she deserved better from her coach. I wanted her to come back and said I would publicly apologize.

He responded, accepted my apology and understood I hadn't intentionally hurt his daughter's feelings. But the damage was done and he said that he thought was best for them not to finish out the season.

I don't judge their decision. I'm fiercely loyal to my kid on the field, so I get it. Maybe he encouraged her to come back she simply didn't want to. I wouldn't have forced my daughter to, either.

This was a season after three all-star girls turned in their paperwork saying they didn't want to be on my team.

I questioned God. Why was this happening?

For the other three girls, each of their reasons had nothing to do with how I treated them. But it didn't matter. My reputation with the board of directors was irreversibly damaged.

In recreation leagues, directors don't ask for letters from parents whose girls' lives have been helped by a coach. Nor, in my case, did the directors give me a chance to explain.

I was embarrassed and deeply hurt.

God said:

My reputation has come under attack, too, unjustly. I knew about this long before you ever signed up as a novice volunteer coach. I hated what it was going to do to your good heart, but I was at work, for you and for those around you. This had to happen for many reasons.

****

So, embarrassed and hurt, I called my friend Mike. "Pick Rachel and I'll help you coach," I told him. I'd rather be head coach, but it wasn't going to happen. So I figured we'd play with Erin and Mike.

Except as I said, Mike didn't draft us.

And he didn't seem too concerned about it either.

I value loyalty above almost anything. Mike didn't owe me anything. Still, on the heels of getting blackballed, which I assume he didn't know, it was salt to the wound.

Another coach drafted Rachel and asked me to help him. We'd coached against each other plenty, but never together. We won the championship that season.

At the end of the year, Mike was making the rounds to see which girls wanted to play all-stars. Rachel was 18 now. I didn't know if she wanted to play again, but I know she'd have liked to have the chance to decide for herself.

But Mike asked and found enough girls to put together a team without ever asking us. What the heck? Twice he had snubbed us. And by this point, I was angry.

I thought back on how Mike had gone through a season of unemployment over the past year and how I'd regularly encouraged him as he struggled through those emasculating times. I was befriended him outside the ballpark. I also knew no other coaches, or fathers, had kept up with him during that time except me.

And for that we get snubbed? Twice?

Prone to stew to a point of holding a grudge, something was pushing me to not let this one lie, and confront him.

I tried to set aside my feelings and let Mike know how I it appeared to me. I had to give him the chance to explain. Maybe there was so grand explanation that I'd not thought of.

So I sent an email, thinking it might be a little weak, but I wanted to phrase my feelings in the right words and I knew I'd fail in person or over the phone. I wrote that when he didn't pick us in the spring I felt betrayed and that I'd miss out on coaching again with a friend. And when he seemingly had gone out of his way not pick us for the all-star team, I concluded that we weren't really friends. Or that he was a lousy excuse for a friend.

"Why'd you do this?" I asked. "I would have involved you, just like I had in the past, in any all-star team. What gives? I thought we were tighter than this."

He read my email, called me and apologized. He said he hadn't really thought about Rachel or me. His apology was sincere. So was his explanation, which frankly stung more. Being intentionally shunned didn't feel much better than not mattering enough to even be considered.

I accepted his apology and told him there were no hard feelings.

That was a lie. There were hard feelings and I was pretty sure that I was done with him. But I was also pretty sure I was done with him.

Whether hard feelings or just self-protection, I'd invested more than my share in this friendship. I'd speak to him if I ever saw him at the fields, but other than that, I was done.

Or so I thought.

God had other plans. The story would really begin a year later.

God said:

You stayed for what was about to come. You just didn't know it. You pushed to keep the relationship alive, but then you were ready to let it die. Sometimes, relationships do fade away. Sometimes, there's a good reason for that. So there is no easy answer for when to let a relationship go except this: Follow my lead.

Chapter 18 – Gone

"A time to be born and a time to die." –
Ecclesiates 3:2

"And this is a God you trust?" – The Enemy

It was Saturday afternoon, May 25, 2013 when I saw the message on Facebook.

"Please pray for my sister Erin!!!! She is only 19. She was perfectly fine and hanging out with me this morning, felt faint and now she is getting brain surgery, and it is not looking good."

I was stunned and immediately sent Mike a text message saying, "Praying for you guys."

He replied and thanked me, and in about five words, told me it was serious.

We exchanged a few texts throughout the day as Mike and Erin's extended family raced to town. Rachel had processed the information to mean this: Erin was going to be in the hospital for a while, recover and then be OK.

Nothing that Mike, or anyone else, told me Saturday directly contradicted that hopeful sentiment. But what I was getting from the texts and Facebook messages sounded far more desperate than encouraging.

"We believe in miracles. We are praying for a miracle," I remember seeing on one post.

On Sunday morning, I got another text: "Erin passed away this morning."

And just like that, she was gone.

****

I can't quite put my finger on the emotion I felt, either initially, or later on. I really could have gone the rest of my life without seeing Erin again, and other than a chance encounter with Mike, she rarely would have crossed my mind.

Obviously, I hurt for Mike and his family. And I did my best to put myself in his shoes, which is sort of the right thing to do, I think, but also somehow selfish, as if I needed to comfort myself in how much I was hurting for Mike.

I had not visited the hospital, which was a mistake. It wasn't because I felt awkward in such settings. On the contrary, that's the ministry I am often called to. I was trying to be respectful to a large gathering of family and felt I wasn't the friend Mike needed in that moment. Maybe I was keeping my distance. I don't know.

And then, Mike called me that night to fill me in on what had happened.

Erin was out shopping with her mom and sister on that Saturday morning and had just eaten breakfast. Mike and Tina had divorced years ago, but Mike was very active in the lives of his girls. After walking out of the restaurant, Erin complained of feeling weird. Then she started vomiting. Then she told her mom she couldn't feel or move the left side of her body.

She faded quickly. By the time she got to the emergency room about 20 minutes later, the damage done to her brain was massive. It was indeed going to take a miracle for her to survive this, doctors told her mom.

Mike got to the hospital within a few minutes. Erin was in a coma, essentially being kept alive on life support.

There was not going to be a miracle. At least not in that E.R., not in the case of Erin O. Matthews, not the way we all had wanted.

Erin was pronounced dead about 24 hours after arriving at the hospital. Mike said he was assured Erin hadn't suffered, and that it was likely an aneurism in her brain, and it had choked out her life within a minute or two.

I mostly just listened and said I was sorry.

The next morning he called again. Would I serve as a pallbearer? Would I be willing to represent the 12 years of Erin's life spent on the softball fields of Lost Mountain?

Softball was a vital part of Erin's life. And for Mike, too. It was their thing to do together every season, the one constant in a father-daughter relationship that was seemingly changing daily.

Would I be the guy to represent that?

This was the real story. Tragic and heartbreaking as it was, this was the story of our relationship. The seven years leading up to this had set the stage for these next few months.

And my role in this story was even larger than representing softball at the funeral. God had chosen me from before time to be Mike's guy during the initial season of loss, whatever that would mean.

I'm not sure what I would need if it were me.

Mike needed Erin's name mentioned, a lot. He wanted her to be remembered. Like a lot of men, he was prone to withdraw into isolation. The stakes had never been like this, though.

In the past, keeping the world at an arm's length and burying himself in busyness and family maintenance seemed a fine way to get through life – even a responsible way. But as we learned together during this time, we're not made to go through life alone. It's impossible to thrive without investing in others and allowing them to invest in you. Yes, grieving is lonely work. But learning to live again after losing a daughter is not a task for one. It really does take a community.

Mike wanted a way out of the darkness of isolation that was threatening to bind him like a mummy. But like most of us, navigating into a place of protection by others was unchartered waters. I could help here. I was called into this, after all. I wasn't sure exactly what that was going to look like, but I was going to be a friend to Mike, a proactive and dependable one at that.

****

Does anything ever look the same in hindsight? I guess not if you're learning from life's events and how you react to them.

I'm glad I was that to Mike. I'm sick about how high and mighty that sounded, though.

I would not have admitted this at the time, chiefly because I didn't recognize it. But throughout my softball years and in my friendship with Mike, I really did believe I was doing a job which others either were not capable of, or not willing, to do.

Paying attention to the hearts of middle school girls was indeed a noble calling. As was being sensitive to things like Mike's jobless state. And I was blameless in all of this. God said so! But that's God being God, seeing me through the blood-red prism of Jesus life, death and resurrection.

But with the benefit of time, I'm convicted (though not condemned) at the realization that I placed, and still do place, expectations on others that were selfish and at times, even smothering. I resented it when others weren't willing to invest what I was willing to invest. I felt entitled for people to feel toward me the way I felt toward them. That was not fair to them and set me up for disappointment.

Was I called into the ministry of softball and the ministry of loving on Mike? Yep. And, both of those callings were opposed by the one who goes to war against my heart every hour of the day. So therein lies my dilemma. How hard do I fight for things that must be fought for and when do I realize that the fight is no longer mine to fight?

God said:

Like I said, it's hard. Follow my lead, and know that when you mess up, my love for you doesn't diminish.

****

But there was one magical day not long after Erin passed away that God reached down and took a softball community into his arms, and held us tightly.

It was Father's Day; the U.S. Open golf tournament was in its final round, with Mickelson in contention. And here, with the humidity high, there were plenty of reasons for a dad to stay at home in a chair, in the air conditioning, watching TV. But one by one, fathers came to the Lost Mountain softball fields.

Hutmacher, Austin and Gouger were there. So were Oliver,

Sennebogen and Johnson. And Malcom, Rhodes and Kuglar. We were all there for one father – Mike Matthews.

We'd all played alongside Mike and we'd played alongside Erin.

And if this could happen to Erin, it could happen to any of our little girls. We wanted to convey that we knew that, and that as a group, we'd do anything we could to help Mike take a step through this hell he was enduring. Erin was Mike's daughter, but in a sense, she was ours, too. We loved her.

At least 60 people were there. Twenty-two of Erin's former teammates played a game in her memory with their dads -- coaches who had donned the WCGS shirts dozens of times over the years.

The game was great, one of the best, with the most talent ever to play on Lost Mountain. Some hadn't played in at least two years, but their skills were on display. After seven innings, we ended at 13-11.

Afterwards, we walked behind the fence on Field 1 where Dave Hutmacher had planted a Japanese maple the day before when it was even hotter. I asked if he'd sweated it out and he joked that he had, and hadn't needed to water it.

That's what love looks like.

With afternoon turning into early evening, we dedicated Erin's tree. And I spoke. I said that today, and from here on, we were all "Team Matthews." I said it was a promise from us to them, that we were brothers and sisters who wanted to play whatever part we could in helping to take care of them and actively love them.

Men shared embraces that said just as much.

And I thought again, this is *what love looks like*.

They missed the U.S. Open, changed plans, played softball in the heart and thanked us letting them give away their Father's Day. They set aside their own work and lives and lived in the moment.

One young woman who had been quite the slugger just a year earlier, now seven months pregnant, took an at-bat that didn't go well, but she played her part. And no one judged. Instead, they delighted in her participation. She was one of ours, too.

We were all one family that day. We were "the church."

I know this now as sure as I'm sitting here writing these words. We experienced true church that day. We were the community of full acceptance and abundant grace. We loved and were loved.

We missed our Erin. But we knew she was watching, laughing and cheering.

And we would see her on the other side.

Late that night, around midnight, I got this email from Mike:

"Thank you so much for today…you have helped preserve some great memories of her and her teammates. Our whole family was touched by the outpouring of kindness and oneness with all of the girls and families."

Oneness. Connection. It's so rare and special you want to hold on while you can. But now I understand that some people play vital, intimate roles for a season, not a lifetime.

I'd never accepted that well. I'd get bitter when friendships faded and assumed I wasn't important enough to them. It was the abandoning.

But there are precious few we will walk through multiple seasons with. That doesn't diminish the essential role of the others, though.

A couple of months earlier, I'd experienced a different kind of loss, the death of a childhood friend – the first girl I'd ever really kissed.

I had seen Carol only once in 25 years. A handful of us from our church youth group had gotten together for a Christmas lunch in 2009, I think. We enjoyed a few memories, but there wasn't the connection I'd hoped for. And that's okay.

At Carol's funeral, I had the chance to remember that she and Jennifer had been the best friends I could have at a time when I was learning so many things for the first time – about love, God's grace and true friendship. I loved them so much. Carol and I dated for what now seems to have been about 10 minutes. It was the summer of 1982. So much of who I am today was born in 1982, but with those friends, I'd found a safe place. I experienced puppy love a couple of times, complete with the heartbreak that followed. But my heart was always handled with care.

And Carol had been our ringleader of goodness. I hadn't thought of her much over 25 years. Yet I realized how high the stakes now were. So much was forever gained in how I emerged from those couple of years, able to love and be loved. I'm so grateful today to all of them, and for Carol, for showing me, and so many others the best of friendships.

As I thought about the impact one good friend can make, a song by Switchfoot, "Souvenirs," spoke to my heart:

> *"I close my eyes and go back in time*
> *I can see you smiling, you're so alive*
> *We were so young, we had no fear*
> *We were so young, we had no idea that life was just*
> *happening*
> *Life was just happening."*

A few hours after Carol's funeral, after the deep introspection of what seemed to be my only time of innocence, I was back at the softball fields. It wasn't a place of innocence anymore, but was still a place where I often recovered pieces of my heart.

Never have I recovered more of my heart than I did that night.

This kid couldn't have been more than 8 years old. But he was armed with a mission, a message and a baseball.

I assume he had a name, but I can't swear to it.

I assume, too, he had a voice. But I didn't hear it.

He wore a red T-shirt. That's the only thing I know for sure.

And at the time, I assumed he probably had parents close by, watching his sister play softball on one of the five West Cobb Girls Softball fields that surrounded the commons area, where players, coaches and parents congregated. Where I was.

He walked up to me while I was talking to another coach. Without saying a word, he stood there long enough for me to glance down at him.

Then he invited me into Life.

Standing three feet in front of me, he tossed me his baseball and immediately retreated about 25 feet and held his glove out.

Now, I'm pretty sure I hadn't given an impression that I was looking for a game of catch. For starters, I didn't have a glove. And I was in the middle of a conversation with another adult.

But when he tossed me the ball and ran to his spot, it was as if he was saying: "It's not that complicated, man. It's a ball. You know what to do with it."

And I did.

For about five minutes, we threw the ball back and forth.

The little boy couldn't have known that these softball fields, for the past 11 years, have been the place where I have felt most alive, the place of my most significant ministry, the place I connected with the next generation, and allowed it to connect with me. The Father knew, though.

William Sanders | 191

And the kid had no idea that just hours earlier, I had been at a funeral for a childhood friend and needed, so badly, for a reminder of those simpler times. But the Father knew where I'd been and what I needed.

Now, I'm usually slow to put it all together. During our impromptu game of toss, I thought it was simply an amusing moment in time. I mean, who does this kid, full of innocence and audacity, think he is anyway? Who does this kind of thing?

Over the course of the next 12 hours, I knew exactly who does this kind of thing.

It was the Someone who knew that the playfulness of my spirit needed wooing on this day. It was the One who knew I needed a taste of the innocence that had been lost. And a reminder of goodness.

We quit when I threw him one last grounder and hollered that I had to go. I'm pretty sure he wasn't going to be the one to quit.

Had he spoken at the end, I now imagine he'd have ended our night with this: "Gotten what you need? Had enough? If not, I've got all night."

Thanks, fella. And thanks Father.

I can't swear to it, but again, with the benefit of time, I'm fairly convinced the kid lived on this earth a total of eight minutes.

God said:

I know the fields were the place of your ministry, where you did My work, and where you and I shared some beautiful moments. I'm proud of how you rallied around Mike when he needed you. Your heart came alive in a new way while ministering to Mike. That was My gift to you in the midst of such sadness. And as for Erin? I can't wait for you to get to see her again. She's the same goofball you remember. She is enjoyed by everyone here. Grieve her loss as long as you need to. But don't hurt for a second for her. She's where she was made for. She's home. Same with Carol.

And the little kid you played toss with after Carol's funeral? You haven't seen him at the fields again, you say? And you never heard him say a word, or see his parents? You never actually touched him? Hmmm. Just remember I love you. And I know what you need, and when you need it, big fella.

Chapter 19 – Healing

"Train up a child in the way he should go; even when he is old he will not depart from it."
– Proverbs 22:6

"You haven't trained her well; you enabled her and crippled her." – The Deceiver

After a couple of years at local colleges, Rachel went away for school in 2013 – and not just away, but six hours away.

"Rachel went away for school." Wow. For at least a decade, I never imagined I'd be able to write such a sentence. This was my little girl who couldn't handle being 50 yards from us. This was the kid who, even after some significant healing, could not spend a single night away from our house or from us. And less than a couple of years removed from that stage of life, here she was heading to the Georgia coast to go to college.

I don't think God could even playfully tell me, *"I told you so,"* because I don't think He ever had told me such. Instead, it was this miraculous gift that had never been promised, but had been longed for, in unspoken ways, for years.

It's not that Jane and I were looking forward to a Rachel-less house. It is that for so long, we'd prayed for a day that she would be able to make it on her own. She first told us she wanted to go away for college only a couple of months before it was to begin. She and her boyfriend of three years had broken up, and she wanted a fresh start in a new place.

Jane helped her apply, seek scholarship money and request various transcripts and records on the off chance that she really would enroll in a college located between Savannah, Georgia and Jacksonville, Florida.

Jane was, and still is, a rock star at running household. She kept track of Rachel and Laura's medications and prayed for Rachel, perhaps on a even or more regular basis than I did. She could not take over the task that Rachel and God had determined was mine. But as I've said, she took care of me, while I took care of Rachel. She was and is a fierce advocate for her children. Had it not been for her accepting her role and playing it to perfection, it all could have crumbled at any minute, including Rachel's hopes of getting into the coastal Georgia college.

Within a few weeks, Rachel got accepted, of course. This small college didn't turn down transfers who'd passed a couple of years of college courses already. But she was too late to get into the dorm. And while many kids would welcome the chance to live off campus, Rachel needed to know there would always be people around. Not getting into the dorm was probably enough to be a deal-breaker.

I'm not always a man of tremendous faith, but I had no doubt that a dorm slot would open for Rachel. Way too much was being orchestrated from above to let a dormitory opening stand in the way of this shot at a miracle.

Sure enough, a space opened. Nothing now was holding her back except the piles of baggage she'd been toting around for most of her life.

"I'm nervous, Dad," Rachel said. "But I want to do this. I'm going to do this."

"You can back out at anytime, ya know," I said.

"Do you think I should back out? Can I not do this?

"No, Rach. I think you should do this and can do this."

"Can you handle me being gone, Dad? I don't want you worrying all the time."

"Are you kidding me? I've prayed for this day for as long as I can remember. How can I not be okay with it?"

Guess what? She did it.

She and her mom drove down on a Friday. I stayed home with Laura, who had auditions for her senior year of drama performances. Everyone – and by everyone, I mean EVERYONE

– assumed I would be a wreck with Rachel leaving. I understood that sentiment, but I firmly believed what I told Rachel was the truth.

And for me, it was an honor to stay home with Laura and provide support for her as she was shimmering and shining with her God-given gift. Laura is as talented of a singer and actress as I've ever seen in a high school kid. I love her every bit as much as I love Rachel. She needed me as much too, just not as acutely or as constantly.

Laura endured Rachel's hell, and the hell that it caused for Jane and me, by becoming emotionally self sufficient at an early age. She never displayed a demanding and acute need for the protection, support and comforting, not like Rachel anyway. So I would be laser-focused on the raging and bright three-alarm fire that was Rachel, while in the bedroom next door, Laura immersed herself into movies, music and sometimes isolation. She's definitely her daddy's daughter.

I don't think I've ever adequately apologized to her for how much more attention I gave to Rachel than I did to her during those years. I think it was what God was calling me to do, spending that intense amount of emotional blood, sweat and tears on Rachel. But like I wrote earlier, He wasn't calling for me to carry every burden and be her God. Had I understood that better, perhaps I would have been a more-attentive father to Laura. But she loves me well, nonetheless. And I love her wildly. And love continues to cover my multitude of sins.

For 19 years, so much of my identity and my being had been consumed by Rachel's wellbeing, and we had such a tight bond that it was logical to assume Rachel leaving would be painfully hard for me. I told Rachel before she left that I could not stand the thought of her being down there, six hours away, if I knew she was miserable, anxious, panicky or depressed. But if she was happy, and if she enjoyed the freedom, the beach and new friends, then I'd not only be OK with her being gone, I'd be giddy. It would be the gift from God that I hadn't even dared to specifically request. How could that not be good?

And for the record, everyone was wrong. I was not a wreck. I basked in it. And I thanked God for it.

Rachel spent a year at the beach college, where she exceeded everyone's expectations. She had moments of anxiety and moments of college limit-testing stupidity. But she made it. That goes into the faith back pocket as well, big time.

She returned home after than year and began a new college, along with Laura, 90 minutes from home. What a great distance 90 minutes from home it for your college kid to be!

God said:

Over and over and over, I told you that I had this. No, I didn't tell you she'd be going to the beach for college in 2013. But I was showing you in so many ways that I really did have plans for Rachel. "For I know the plans I have for Rachel. They are plans

198 | *STAYING*

for good and not for disaster, to give her a future and a hope."
Remember that verse. Jane clung to it more than you did, but it
wasn't a competition, and I wasn't keeping track of how many
times you or Jane quoted it. But the plans were there all along. I
imagine you'd have chosen an easier path for Rachel. I'm sure
you'd have chosen a simpler childhood for yourself, too. But just
like you can now see how much Rachel was going to need a father
who'd been broken and battered to the point of tenderness, in time,
you and Rachel will see how I'm using the hardships she's
endured. There will be more bumps in the road. You know that by
now. It's the world you live in. But remember, I got this. Nothing
will ever spiral out of control because I am in control. Oh, and I
gave you Laura. And I gave you to Laura. She is the bomb on
stage, isn't she? She knows how much you love her. And so do I.
But go tell her again. And then again. And then again.

Chapter 20 –
Meeting Aunt Claire

"Then you will know the truth, and the truth will set you free." – John 8:32

"You really want to know how screwed up four family is, how screwed up you are? I can't wait."
– The Deceiver

I was several months into writing this book before I began to see the crater-size holes in my story. I knew I'd get to this point. I knew those holes were there. But until I got some of the more basic questions answered, I didn't know how to find these more complex questions, much less discover the answers.

I realized I had to take my second big risk. The first one was talking this through with Dad, and that was risky only because of what it might do to our relationship, and what I thought it might do to him.

But the second risk would involve going beyond him to gather the missing pieces that he couldn't provide.

No one on my dad's side of the family had even had contact with anyone from Charlotte's side since those brief encounters in 1980 when she came on Mother's Day to show me who my real mother was, and when she and her sister Claire showed up at Cindy's high school graduation a couple of weeks later.

Growing up, just the thought of the Burns side of the family was scary. I equated that name with fear, abduction and abandonment, a dark closet I didn't go into. Even now, pushing 50, I have to muster up a surprising amount of courage to contact Claire, Charlotte's only surviving sister.

It wasn't like I'd be contacting Charlotte herself – not by a long shot. But since finding out Charlotte had died in 2004, Claire was the only person left who could answer my questions. And I had plenty.

Was she schizophrenic? Is there a psychiatric history, perhaps genetic, that I need to let my doctors know about? Did she ever ask about me? Did she ever really love us?

I have no memories of Claire. Cindy has some, and they were mostly pleasant. And Dad spoke highly of her when I told him I had decided to contact her. Best we knew, she hadn't been a part of the whole abandonment/abduction period. She'd only been a teenager at the time.

As I was deciding how to approach her, I thought of her as Switzerland. She hadn't done anything wrong in 1971, but she hadn't done a whole lot since then to make it right, either. And our situation had, for years, seemed to call for something more than a Switzerland approach from anybody who possibly could have gotten in Charlotte's ear.

I had no reason to think Claire didn't have at least some access to Charlotte. I figured her showing up at Cindy's graduation with her was evidence enough. It had been more than 30 years ago, but it was my last point of reference.

It didn't take me long to locate Claire and to get an email address and a phone number. She lives 90 minutes from me. I called Cindy and Dad to let them know of my plans, wondering if they'd object, and not sure what I would do if they did. But I didn't anticipate that. By now, everyone was ready to rip off this tattered Band-Aid of silence and hiding and see what would happen.

I paced my den upstairs for a while and finally sent Claire a note. Unlike the one I sent my dad, that contained 20 questions that I fired off one after the other, I asked Claire only one question: one question. "Are you willing to tell me about Charlotte?"

Two hours later, at 6 p.m. exactly I got a response.

"I am so glad to hear you are alive and well! I have always felt so sad about not knowing you and Cindy. I am happy to answer any questions you may have about Charlotte. She was interesting to say the least! Sorry to say I was not always too congenial with her myself. I look forward to filling you in as much as I can – no strings attached!"

We agreed to talk by phone on Friday, two days later. I took a personal day from my job, figuring if all went well, it would be a long conversation and a good day to write. If it went poorly? Probably best to be at home for that too.

In my 20-plus years working for daily newspapers, I have done hundreds, if not thousands, of interviews. I know how to interview subjects with a professional detachment. Even the ones I was most sympathetic toward, I always worked to focus on the story and not get caught up in the personal elements of the story. I had no doubt I'd do the same when I talked to Claire. What I didn't know was whether I'd believe her or not. The wonderful first impression notwithstanding, I had little idea what kind of person she was. I envisioned no scenario that could move me to any particular emotion.

I realize now how crazy that sounds.

****

Come Friday morning, I retreated to my den to steel myself for whatever I might hear. Thirty-six hours later, I still didn't expect for this to be emotional, but beyond a bout of defensiveness or two I expected she'd express toward her sister, I believed I could be okay with that, too.

But somewhere between our first exchange and Friday, a thought occurred to me: What if I heard something revealing or negative about Dad? What if I found out he was hiding some things too? That could disorient me, cause me some distress and I might not recover well enough to continue with my questions. I was still thinking of it as detached as I could, like I was conducting a professional interview. But this new possibility could derail everything.   So I did have some steeling of self to do. I sat down, alone with a cup of black coffee, and began to pray.

Only the words didn't come.

I sat there for a few more minutes, asking myself what it was, specifically, that I was hoping to get out of this call. That was a problem, because I didn't know specifically what I was hoping to learn.

Then I pondered, "What would success from this phone call look like?' And with that question came clarity.

I looked at my cell phone – 9:19 a.m. I uttered this one-sentence prayer:

"Lord, let this phone call matter, and let it matter for good."

At 9:20 a.m., I made the call.

"Hello, Claire."

I offered nothing else, not yet. No small talk, no nothing. Just, "Hello, Claire."

She would have to fill the void. And she did.

"Hi, Bill. Since your email, I have been thinking, 'How can I talk to you and not hurt you, tell you things about Charlotte that you won't want to hear and yet tell it like it is?' I'm just going to lay it out there and hope God will take care of your heart."

And with those words, we were off. For two hours and 10 minutes, I mostly listened, not even needing to ask many of the questions I'd typed out. In between that introductory email and this phone call, I had followed up with another email, listing a few topics on which I knew I wanted to hear from her.

I thought my questions were good ones. After all, I had spent 20 years coming up with questions and asking them of people. In hindsight I was missing the most obvious one. My first question should have been: "What can you tell me about Charlotte that I would have never dreamed of asking?" That would have been a good place to start, because there were plenty of things I would have never dreamed of asking.

Everything my dad had told me about Charlotte being manipulative, money hungry and deceitful were true – times 10. And based on Claire's accounts of their childhood, those characteristics shone through long before Dad got caught up in her web.

Their aunt, Margaret Burns, was a psychiatrist and the second woman ever to graduate from Duke University School of Medicine. She remained a big deal in the psychiatric community in North Carolina for decades. Claire and Margaret became close later in life, and Margaret was able to offer some perspective on Charlotte's early years and how those might have set her on a destructive course.

When Gan (Alice) was 20, she gave birth to Charlotte. Mr. Burns had been in the Navy during World War II. He was stationed in Hawaii for a stretch of time. When he was home, he was a strict disciplinarian. But when he wasn't, Charlotte and her mother lived with their grandparents in a home facing East Lake Country Club's golf course, one of Atlanta's most prestigious neighborhoods.

Charlotte was the first grandchild and, in her grandparent's eyes, could do no wrong. It scared me how similar that sounded to how I was treated by Nana.

Aunt Margaret believed the adoration Charlotte got from her grandparents created an unrealistic expectation she would have about how her dad would see her and treat her. According to Claire, Mr. Burns did not convey that kind of adoration. He was stolid with high standards of discipline and believed in not sparing the rod.

Charlotte and Claire both grew to like it when their dad was gone because everything was easier. When he'd return home, apparently there was hell to pay if one of his girls talked back to their mom or even looked at her wrong.

Claire became emotionally close to her dad in adulthood. But as a child, she saw him for what he was – an iron-fisted, no-nonsense disciplinarian.

"I was scared to death of him," Claire said. "I looked forward to him not being there because we could relax and maybe be late from time to time without fear of being knocked across the side of the room. We would dread sitting at the dinner table because mom would tell dad all the bad things we'd done, and he spanked us and spanked us hard. I now would call it abuse."

By the time Charlotte was 15 or so, she had begun to rely on her looks, her ability to control a room and her skill at lying. She was promiscuous, sneaky and often convinced Claire to cover for her. She had become resentful toward their dad to the point of hating him, Claire believes.

Charlotte was a good student, though, and sailed through high school and enrolled at the University of Georgia. It was there that she met Mary Ellen, a resident assistant on the dorm floor where Charlotte lived.

Mary Ellen was a burgeoning alcoholic and a lesbian. Away from her dad's house, Charlotte had the freedom to explore.

"Charlotte was not a lesbian," Claire said. "She once told me she was bisexual. To me, she was just promiscuous."

The Burns family got its introduction to Mary Ellen's influence one day when they stopped in Athens, Ga., to pick up a defiant Charlotte and take her with them to Asheville, N.C., where Mr. Burns' parents were celebrating their 50th wedding anniversary. Charlotte had told her dad she didn't want to go. First she said she had too much schoolwork. Then she said she was sick. Mr. Burns got madder with every excuse and showed up unannounced to "drag her to the car by her scalp, if necessary," Claire said.

What he found was Charlotte in Mary Ellen's dorm room, in her bed and under the covers. Mary Ellen was making excuses, but Mr. Burns knew what was going on, and it didn't jibe with his Presbyterian/military ways – particularly not in the early '60s.

Some time later, Charlotte met my dad at a fraternity party. She eventually got pregnant with his child and get married. But one thing she didn't get over was the allure of Mary Ellen, and that would play out soon after Cindy and I were born.

Charlotte was a horrible wife to my dad, and this was not only according to him. Dad still doesn't talk about Charlotte other than to say she held custody over his head all the time and that she wanted material things he couldn't provide.

But Claire saw how bad Charlotte was to Dad, as did Jan, their baby sister, who was nine years younger than Claire, but became her best friend. Jan died at 27 from a pulmonary embolism following years of illness.

"After they were married, Jan and I would talk about how mean Charlotte was," Claire said. "She was mean as a snake. I'm not sure how your dad handled it. She was bossy and could get an awful look on her face and would be demanding of him. He became her doormat and gopher. He was living in guilt for having gotten her pregnant. To me, your dad was in an abusive relationship that I think almost killed him."

I have begun to understand the depths of the pain Dad went through after the abandonment and abduction. But until talking to Claire, I didn't grasp the hell he endured. He allowed himself to take some of the worst mental and emotional abuse for the sake of his children. Perhaps that's why he felt the shame for years.

"Everything I did was because of you and Cindy," Dad said. "I wasn't going to let you get stuck living with her. I was willing to stay married until you both were out of high school."

Eighteen more years just to protect Cindy and me?

Regardless of the reasoning, is there any greater love than to *lay down* your life?

After Cindy was born, my dad and Charlotte moved the family, to Charlotte, North Carolina. Charming and engaging when she wanted to be, my mom had made friends and involved herself at enough social settings in Atlanta that Mary Ellen's pull wasn't strong. But when we moved, she had no friends and no status, and it didn't take long for Mary Ellen to re-emerge.

After at least two weeklong stints in which Mary Ellen was at our house, Charlotte left 8-year-old Cindy and me with a neighbor and flew to Tampa, never to return.

"As far as Jan and I were concerned, divorce would have been fine," Claire said. "Even lesbianism would have been... understandable, I guess. But abandoning your children? We were in disbelief that anyone, much less someone related to us, could do that. It was beyond my ability to even fathom."

Despite plenty of signs over the years, Claire, Jan and her parents were not convinced that Charlotte was having an affair with Mary Ellen. They, particularly Mr. Burns, were holding onto hope that this time, unlike so many other times, she wasn't lying to them.

Walking out on Cindy and me was the final straw in Claire's mind. But apparently Charlotte's skill at conniving convinced her mom and dad to hold out hope. So a few months later when Charlotte kidnapped us, her mother Alice was her accessory.

According to Claire, it was the biggest regret of Alice's life. Though Claire never forgave Charlotte for the hurt she caused, she did forgive her mom for her part in the kidnapping. But even that took some time.

"The only way I could get to a place of forgiveness for my mom is realizing that she, and really all of us, were too stupid to not see how badly we were being manipulated and lied to."

Mr. Burns came to the same realization on January 18, 1973, around lunchtime.

That was the day we were all in court, where my fate was going to be determined by the court "then and there."

Mr. Burns was one of the men invited into Judge Williams' chambers that morning.

"I remember my dad saying that was when he realized he'd been hoodwinked," Claire said. "He had been paying for her lawyer this whole time, and all the while, he kept asking Charlotte if there were things he needed to know."

"Tell me the truth, Charlotte," Mr. Burns said.

"I am, Daddy. I promise," Charlotte replied.

After seeing the letters and finding out the truth, Claire said: "From then on, he washed his hands of her. He was polite to her after that, and even let her and (her second husband) Mac live in a cabin on their property for a time. But their relationship was irrevocably damaged. It was like he had no love left for her."

Claire also knew what my dad knew, that Charlotte never wanted Cindy and me in her Tampa life.

"Charlotte had no real desire for the responsibility of being a mother. She was determined that your dad would not have you either, though. That's how mean she was. She blamed our parents for not stepping in and somehow adopting you themselves, which was, of course, just another way of trying to control my parents through guilt," Claire said.

Eventually, Charlotte grew tired of Mary Ellen's alcoholism and returned to Georgia. Mary Ellen died on November 13, 1987, in Tampa, from her alcoholism. She had recently been fired from her job as a school counselor in Hillsborough County, Florida.

Once back in Georgia, Charlotte met Bud McCallum, a man 15 years her elder. Claire describes him as a sad, poor man, a recovering alcoholic, who had bad teeth, little education and zero polish. Charlotte and Bud married around 1978 and lived near Claire. Bud became part of the family, sort of, Claire said.

Charlotte treated Bud like she'd treated my dad. She couldn't hold custody over him, though. But she could hold alcohol over him. Soon after they married, Bud, who'd been sober for years, began drinking again. He divorced Charlotte three years later and moved to Indiana. Then, in a turn of events almost beyond belief, he found Charlotte in bed with his son, Richard, who was about 24 years old at the time. The shock was the final -- and possible fatal -- straw for Bud. He died a year later.

Maybe Claire was right. Maybe my dad was lucky to get out alive. Mary Ellen didn't. Mac didn't. Richard did, but only with the knowledge that he'd slept with his stepmother, who later became his wife.

Yes, Charlotte and Richard McCallum married sometime after 1988, a time in which she was introducing him as her stepson and then going home and sharing a bed with him. She wouldn't acknowledge the marriage publicly for years. As was the case much of his life, Mr. Burns was hoping against all the logic in his mind that what he knew in his heart to be true was wrong.

During the last year of his life, with his health declining, he would ask Claire at least weekly whether she'd been able to find out if Charlotte and Richard were married. She had not been able to find proof, she told him.

Keep looking. Keep investigating. Find out the truth, once and for all, for a dying man.

Several months after Mr. Burns died, Claire found out the truth. Charlotte had indeed married the son of her ex-husband. Mr. Burns apparently had let his heart win out over his head in the end. In his will, he left a trust fund that would provide for Charlotte's living expenses until she succumbed to lung cancer. But once Charlotte was dead, there'd be nothing for Richard.

Charlotte was not appeased.

"When the executor of the estate told Charlotte that, it was the last time she ever talked to me. I went to her memorial service years later and saw Richard. We were both cordial. I haven't seen him since."

God said:

"And now you know. And more today than ever, I want you to let it go and be healed of it forever. You have more reason to hate today than you've ever had. Don't. It's wasted energy. In fact, it's worse than wasted energy. I loved Charlotte as much as I loved you. I died for Charlotte. But she made her choices. And she stood before me in judgment. And it is settled. You needed to come to that place too. Now you need to dwell on the good that I have done and am still doing with this. It's time to realize the past can't hurt you, it can only empower you when you press on with me toward the high calling."

Chapter 21 – Grieving

"There is a time for everything, and a season for every activity under the heavens; a time to weep and a time to laugh, a time to mourn and a time to dance." – Ecclesiastes 3:1, 4

"What you've learned will come back to bite you. It won't set you free. I'll find new ways to make it bind you." – The Deceiver

I shared Claire's story with Cindy and then my dad. It was vindication for both, whether they wanted it or not. Neither Cindy nor I felt guilt about not reaching out to Charlotte to extend our forgiveness. Had we not found out the whole truth, some day we might have.

Have I found out all there is to know about Charlotte? Probably not. Life's a journey, and now that I've unlocked those doors and walk freely in the paths of those who knew Charlotte all of her life, I'll probably hear more, but I can't imagine I will learn more.

It took decades for my sister, Dad and me to be ready for me to open these doors. Even now, I'm not sure Cindy and Dad are really ready for it. But the reservoirs from which I can dip for information on Charlotte are drying up, so the time is now.

Claire was a goldmine of information I almost didn't explore. What she told me cemented in my mind that not reaching out to Charlotte over the years, at the very least, wasn't poor judgment on my end. And it also showed me, as she puts it, that Claire was "on our team the whole time." Who knew?

She had made just one evident mistake, showing up with Charlotte at Cindy's high school graduation in 1980. For that, and the small fear and discomfort it caused, she said she was sorry. Charlotte had "hoodwinked" her once again into believing she had changed. She hadn't as the subsequent years would show.

Common sense leads me to assume Charlotte had some good in her. And I don't mean charm or being good at working a room. No one denied that she had those skills. But I assume she had good in her that gave her some desirable qualities. For instance, she was able to hold down a job at an Atlanta hospital for quite some time. Maybe she was a good worker.

I simply didn't know her. I don't remember any good things about her as a mother. And I didn't hear good things about her as a wife. When I talked to Claire, I didn't hear anything about her being a good daughter or a good sister. When I talked to

Claire's daughter, Dawn, I didn't hear of her being a good aunt. Could mental illness be at the root of all this? When I think of the most horrific criminals of the past 50 years – Dahmer, Bundy, the guy who kept three young women chained in his basement in Ohio – I can't help but think they suffered from some severe mental and emotional disease. But so do millions of other people.

A sociopath is antisocial, often criminal, and lacks a sense of moral responsibility or social conscience. A psychopath is antisocial with a similarly diminished level of empathy and remorse, but who acts out with "disinhibited" and bold behavior.

As far as I could tell, Charlotte was equal parts sick and mean from long before she met my dad. She was sick and mean throughout the abandonment, abduction, affairs and incestuous lifestyle. She was sick and mean to her parents, sisters and anyone who risked taking a chance on her.

And she died that way on June 11, 2004. The next day, June 12, 2004, was the first day in 50 years Charlotte wasn't hurting someone. That's a horrible, haunting legacy to leave.

There's a temptation to soften this to take the edge off, to edit Claire's words about her sister. In fact, I chose not to include everything I learned. And I don't like writing that "she died sick and mean." I'd like to appear above any lasting bitterness or anger and come across as a healthy, well-adjusted father and husband.

But I can't mince words. I can't be less than accurate, not after going to such great lengths to be honest God hasn't called me to be a nice guy. He's called me to stay and to forgive.

216 | *STAYING*

I can say without reservation that while lots of bad stuff has happened to me and to those I love–real, unmistakable and lasting hurt–God has made good on his promise to bring about good from all the bad. Every. Single. Time.

Why was all the hurt necessary? I don't know. Was it necessary? I guess. I can't say for sure. We live in a fallen world and God allows us to suffer for a number of reasons, none of which should be construed as Him being mad at us, or not loving us.

I haven't given this a lot of thought, but what if things had gone the other way? If Dad wasn't a stayer, or if the courts got it wrong, or if Charlotte had simply evaded authorities for years? What would my life have looked like?

My dad, who is quick to admit he made mistakes and squirms at the notion of being heroic, said we wouldn't have survived with Charlotte. Claire said the same, almost to the word.

It's all speculative. But it is worth recognizing that we were rescued from something that might have proved unrecoverable. For that, I say thank you, Lord.

Here's something else I haven't spent time thinking about before. What would I say to Charlotte if could speak to her today? This one deserves more attention.

I think I would say something like this:

"I'm finally learning my story. I'm learning more about myself, about Cindy and Dad and in your sickness, your meanness, and your selfish ignorance, what you did to us.

"I haven't thought about you much. But somewhere below the conscious level, you were never far from my psyche. What you did – and didn't do – had a huge impact on me. I'm just now figuring that out. And it's not good, Charlotte. You stole my childhood and you played the single biggest role in me growing up afraid and unsure of myself.

"I never hated you growing up. I simply didn't give enough energy or thought to it. But when I finally realized what you stole from me, and the role you played in me growing up without many of the things a boy needs, I found that hatred.

"But by reaching the point of hate, I finally can grieve what you robbed from me. And by doing that, I can begin to truly forgive. That's the best I can offer you, Charlotte. And that makes you a part of my life for the first time in 40 years."

****

For a while, I thought this was as far as God was asking me to go in forgiving or trying to understand Charlotte.

But I was wrong.

For the first time ever, I thought:

God created her the same way he created me, in His image, fearfully and wonderfully.

What, then, went so awry in her heart and in her mind?

I know the biblical answer. We are born into sin and into a world that is not the home in which we were intended to live. I know we all have hearts of stones that need to be replaced by hearts of flesh that comes by knowing Jesus.

I do not minimize those central truths at all. But what did Mr. Burns contribute in his absence and tough fathering style – something we might call abusive today? I'd previously never given thought to that. And while I don't know to what degree it affected her, it had to play some role, probably a significant one.

I'm learning how her actions, as well as those of my dad, played such a huge role in shaping who I became. How can I think her upbringing didn't play an equally big role in shaping her life?

So my paradigm begins to shift.

Mr. Burns, by being at least somewhat of an abandoner, at least somewhat of an abusive father, begat a full-fledged abandoning and abusive daughter.

And purely the grace of God, in me, it begat the opposite – one so affected by the stark contrast between abandoning and staying, that instead of running, I clung.

Free will, poor choices and personal responsibility play a big role too, of course. God did not create Charlotte and then put her in a situation where there was no chance for her to choose righteousness, goodness and love. Sick and broken as she might have been, she made some incredibly poor choices that affected generations of Sanders family members.

I don't get to know all the answers. But to deal with this kind of wounding, do I need to know the exact extent of her mental illness vs. pure meanness?

My initial response is no.

Can I write it all off as individual responsibility, and not give weight to the fact that perhaps she was a helpless victim of a sick mind?

Yep. I can. But should I?

Should you, in your story?

One of John Eldredge's central themes in *Wild at Heart* is that things are not always as they seem. He prays for eyes to see with clarity. So do I.

Grieving an unconscionable loss of innocence isn't a once-and-done thing. It's not a one-season, go-through-the-steps-and-you're-good sort of thing, either. Time won't heal all wounds. But healing is available, and time is almost always a tool used by God in the healing process.

For four decades, I thought none of this mattered. Then I thought it would consume me. Then I thought I'd dealt with it, with God. Then I saw residue that remained, so I scrubbed that away.

But then there was an itch that had to be scratched. And when I did, it felt great, like scratching always does. Until I rubbed it raw and it started to bleed again.

Healing is a process. Often, God doesn't show up the way we would like and fix the things in our lives and hearts that so deeply need fixing. Theologically speaking, I get this and trust his goodness and providence. But when we're in the midst of it, and God seemingly isn't showing up, clinging to that theological truth feels a lot like hanging onto Jell-O. It's why religious platitudes fall flat when talking to a mom whose son just died of cancer.

So, don't cling to theology. Get close to Jesus and let him cling to you. There will be times when your grip on theology will simply be too exhausting. You won't even have the strength to hang onto Jesus. It's why we need a Savior. He'll hang on to us.

Ultimately, why Charlotte was the way she was doesn't matter. It matters that God was the way He was.

Having finally grieved and then hated Charlotte for what she did to me, and then getting to forgiveness, I now spend no time judging her or her actions.

Maybe she was a helpless victim of a chemical imbalance, a strained daddy-daughter relationship and confused soul who didn't have as much say-so over her actions as I've always assumed she did.

Maybe she simply stole Cindy and me for money, never knew how to love us and was largely an awful, self-centered person.

I'm OK with that, too.

And that's no small miracle.

God said:

I alone am judge and jury. I've got that covered. I'm proud of you for grieving what was taken from you, for honestly assessing your relationship with Charlotte and for helping your dad and Cindy recover a little more of their hearts too. It was all on my perfect timing. And remember this: Nothing is ever over and done with.

Chapter 22 – Sunset

"See, I am making all things new!" – Rev. 21:5

"You think you can trust your heart to God? Don't be a fool. And you don't have to trust me about this either. Just look inside yourself." – The Deceiver

The sun has set on the lives of many of those directly affected by the events of 1971. Nana and Pop, Charlotte and her parents, Mary Ellen and Mac McCallum are all gone.

The rest of us have fewer days ahead than behind.

After I found out everything I set out to know and then some, and after Dad and I reached a new level of trust and intimacy, even after God spoke truth into the events of my childhood, adolescence and parenthood, I didn't sense I was finished. Something, or someone, was gently urging me to go further. Was it just my journalistic instincts running in high gear?

Was it God speaking to me? I'm not sure. When He speaks, it's usually in a still, small voice. Maybe I just wasn't quiet enough yet to hear him.

When I set out to research and write my story, I stated that it would have been worthwhile if it brought my dad more good than hurt. And it needed to be by a wide margin. I think it has done that, but I needed to ask him to make sure. He told me that it was.

Still, much like I wish I could go back and talk to Charlotte, I wish I could speak some truth to my 30-year-old dad, right before our world was about to explode.

With 20/20 hindsight, I'd tell Dad this:

"You have what it takes to go through what you're about to endure. Not many do. You are going to show me what it means to be a stayer, and while this might not make sense to you yet, know that Cindy and I are going to turn out just fine.

"But Dad, steel yourself. The hurt you're about to feel is going to knock you off your feet. There will be times when it will look hopeless. But it never is.

"The best news I can give you: We'll all be around 40 years from now, and the time will be right to talk this through."

****

I had told Claire in my first email that I was looking for answers about Charlotte and that I wasn't looking for any kind of relationship. And I meant it. But I meant it because of fear – I was afraid. And it wasn't a rational fear. It was an instinctual one, one that had burrowed inside me from the time I was a little boy.

My rational thinking asked what harm could Charlotte's sister do to me, or my family, even if she was more like Charlotte than I thought? But my instinctual fear was telling me I didn't need a rational reason, and that I should keep Claire and anyone on that side of the family at well more than an arm's length.

Then I wondered, what if God had brought me through this safe and intact for a whole host of reasons? And what if one of them was to fully and truly offer Claire forgiveness and to let her know her nephew?

God doesn't want instinctual, irrational fear to be the motivating force behind anything we do. I've let that kind of fear rule my actions for too long. If I could trust that God would take care of me, and my family, maybe He could lead us to further healing.

Would God orchestrate this whole thing to bring Dad and me closer? Or to let Claire wash away the residue of guilt and shame? Of course He would. And He reminded me of that just last week.

When my family and I moved back to the Atlanta area in 1997, we began attending Roswell Street Baptist Church. I had grown up in that church, my sister and her family were there, so it seemed logical. In our two years there, we made no real friends, invested in no one's life and made no emotional deposits or withdrawals. In terms of a church-going experience, it was two wasted years of our lives.

Except for this: One Sunday morning, a man named Fernando Ortega was the guest soloist. He sung a song titled *Jesus, King of Angels*. And it made enough of an impact on me that I bought his CD, having no idea *it* would become an anthem of hope for Rachel and me.

Many nights during Rachel's worst years, right before bedtime, she and I would lie on the living room floor, with her boom box and my CD. We'd listen to the song as I held her. The words were my prayer for her.

> *Jesus, King of angels, heaven's light*
> *Shine Your face upon this house tonight*
> *Let no evil come into my dreams*
> *Light of heaven, keep me in Your peace*
> *Remind me how You made dark spirits flee*
> *And spoke Your power to the raging sea*
> *And spoke Your mercy to a sinful man*
> *Remind me, Jesus, this is what I am.*
> *The universe is vast beyond the stars*
> *But You are mindful when the sparrow falls*
> *And mindful of the anxious thoughts*
> *That find me, surround me and bind me.*
> *Jesus, King of angels, heaven's light*
> *Hold my hand and keep me through this night.*

Ortega's soft, smooth voice soothed us both. But the words gave us hope that peace and terror-free nights would come. It took a lot of nights, but they did come. And eventually, they stayed.

It wasn't until a few weeks ago – more than a decade after I heard him sing – that God gave me a glimpse of how He'd worked in this crisis. I probably would have never heard of Fernando

Ortega had it not been for that Sunday. I'd have never heard the song and I'd not have spent those nights with Rachel in my arms, praying those words over her.

I would have prayed regardless – and perhaps using a different song. But while Ortega didn't write it specifically for Rachel and me, he might as well have.

And that is my assurance today, from a heart plucked out of darkness.

God moved through a man and his song.

And now I know He is a God who would move in this way. Maybe He was setting up to do something similar for Dad. For Cindy. For Claire. For all of us who'd receive it.

With that realization, in a matter of a few weeks, 40-plus years of distrust in the Burns name had essentially dissolved – in me, in Cindy and in Dad.

I asked Claire if I could talk to one of her daughters, my cousin, another term I never thought I'd use. I wanted her take on Charlotte and wondered what she remembered. Had it all seemed as strange to them, growing up with no clue about our side of the family?

Claire said, "Sure. Talk to Dawn. She'll be thrilled to get a chance to tell you what she knows. Here's her number and email address. But she works during the day at a school here in Gainesville, she said. So wait until late afternoon or early evening."

This was one in a line of potentially gulp-inducing moments. It is the same school where my stepsister Amy teaches. And it's where her four daughters attend school. The world that had already gotten significantly smaller when learning that Claire lived in Gainesville and had seen my dad at church one Sunday just got reduced to a laughable size. Dawn and Amy probably knew each other. It got even more intimate than that. Dawn is one of my niece's teachers. And guess whom she saw during Grandparent's Day at the school?

"When your dad came to Grandparent's Day, we shook hands as though we had just met," Dawn said. "I am not sure we made direct eye contact. I tried not to because I am sure I would not have held it together, as well. I wanted very much to reach out and hug him and let him know I am not Charlotte!

"I guess there is some embarrassment on my part, wishing your dad could know that the Burns family was truly a fine, loving and respected family. I guess there is also part of me that is so sorry that your dad felt so much pain as a result of Charlotte's misbehavior. It breaks my heart to think about it."

I called Mom and Dad.

"Guys, there's one more little twist," I told them, before sharing with them what Dawn had told me.

It wasn't lost on me, or anyone else on my side of the family that ne of my nieces was being taught by the niece of the woman who abducted Cindy and me. And my niece is the same age as I was when I was taken.

But because of the seismic shift in how we all viewed that side of the family, peace ruled.

Mom and Dad could not have been more touched by Dawn's sensitivity and thoughtfulness. That, along with Amy telling them she is a terrific teacher and such a kind person, melted any tension or anxiety.

Mom and Dad were fine with letting Claire and Dawn know all about their lives. That wouldn't have been the case a before. It wouldn't have been fathomable.

And Cindy, while fine with me doing whatever I felt I needed to do, was adamant that no further good would come from her making contact with anyone on the Burns' side of the family. She was glad I had told them that she harbored no ill will towards them, and that was good enough.

Only it wasn't. As the glaciers of distrust and fear melted at a tropical pace, Cindy changed her mind, too, and emailed Dawn:

"Never in a million years did I think I would be able to be in touch with you! Stunned and amazed are the only two words I can come up with right now. I tried to answer some of Bill's questions and help with timelines when he was starting, but being a kid myself at the time of the events. I wasn't a huge resource for those kinds of specifics. What I had were clear and vivid memories of you, Dana and my Aunt Claire, and desperately wishing I was your sister and that your mom was my mom. I always felt loved and cared for with y'all."

On March 17, 2014, on an unusually cold, gray, wet St. Patrick's Day morning I got in my car and began the 90-minute drive to Gainesville, Georgia, to visit with Claire and Dawn for the first time in more than four decades.

The first picture of Charlotte I saw on this visit – the first one I'd probably ever seen of her older than 30 – knocked the wind out of me, but only for a second or two. There was no date stamp, but I was told it was taken sometime in the early to mid '90s. I saw about a half dozen other ones, all from roughly the same years, and had no reaction.

But the first one startled me. For a second or two, Charlotte leaped off the picture album and stared straight back at me. I had not anticipated having a reaction, but probably because I hadn't given any thought as to whether I'd have a reaction.

Charlotte stared at me as if to say: "That's right boy. Whatcha got to say for yourself?"

Am I reading more into those two seconds than I should? Maybe. But maybe those two seconds gave me a hint of what I would expect from Charlotte if she were standing in front of me today.

For the three hours I spent with Claire and Dawn – the sister and the niece – I heard nothing good about Charlotte except that she was smart – duplicitous and manipulatively smart, of course. But book smart too. In the months of research and interviews, never have I heard the word "kind." Or giving. Or selfless. Or even misunderstood. Not once. Maybe if I had cast a wider net, I'd have found people who would have used those words. But they weren't forthcoming from those who knew her best.

Like I wrote, it was only the first picture that affected me. But I learned a fair amount from another. It was of Mr. Burns, during that same time period, with his arm around Charlotte. I might not have noticed, had Dawn not directed me to it. But the look on Mr. Burns' face, while having his arm around his eldest daughter, was about the same look I'd have if she was alive, and I was forced to put my arm around her.

It was a sad, joyless, beaten face that could not wait for the camera to click so he could get some separation from Charlotte.

"He didn't love her after that day in court," Claire reminded me. "He tolerated her. The switch had been flipped in an instant that day."

Could I ever get to that place with Rachel or Laura, where I no longer loved them? I can't envision that possibility; I won't even try. Yet if Claire had said right the opposite, that Mr. Burns just kept on loving his daughter, even when she continued to disappoint him, I don't think I would have liked the sound of that, either.

Charlotte put her father in a no-win situation in the eyes of many, including me. He was damned if he did, damned if he didn't. She forced him into a life where it was impossible for me, or the rest of my family, to respect him. And while I can't find anyone to use words like compassionate and loving in regard to Charlotte, the Burns' side of the family says those are the exact words that best describe Mr. Burns. And I believe them. It is unfortunate he was so hopelessly damned in our eyes.

****

About a month later, Cindy came to Atlanta on a Thursday.

"Wanna ride up to Gainesville on Friday to see Amy and her kids?" I asked.

She did.

"Want me to call Claire and Dawn and see if they want to meet us for a cup of coffee?"

Cindy and I had talked about whether she'd close the circle at some point and meet with Claire and Dawn in person. She figured she probably would, but hadn't counted on it happening so quickly. Matters such as this, to Cindy, usually require serious ruminating.

"I don't know. I'm not sure I'm ready," she said.

"I think we should. They'll be thrilled to see you, we can keep it to an hour, and the timing is right. It's not forced right now. It might seem forced a year from now, but it's fresh on all of our minds right now."

Without that rumination time, Cindy agreed. Rumination, mind you, wouldn't have worked in my favor on this. And I wanted them to meet, mostly for the right reasons, but also the journalist in me wanted to observe how it played out.

We drove up Friday and met them at a Wendy's restaurant. We got there first. We walked around the fast-food restaurant, seemingly aimlessly, looking for a table that felt right. Yeah, we were in a Wendy's, looking for a table that felt right.

We chose our table, too close to the front and to a door to have the right feeling. But it would have to do. We sat on the same side of the table and waited. Cindy was nervous. I imagine Dawn and Clarie were, too. For once, I was in the catbird's seat, being the one that stood out for being at ease.

I saw them drive up in Claire's SUV.

"There they are," I said.

"I'm going to throw up," Cindy said.

"You're not going to throw up. You're not going to have an anxiety attack. You'll be fine."

"I know… But I think I'm going to throw up."

"Too late. They're walking in."

I had told Cindy that the reunion was going to be 100 times easier than she was imagining. It's hard and weird to try to catch up on 45 years of life in 45 minutes. There is so much to say, but also the constricting reality that there's only so much anyone *can* say.

Everyone hugged. Claire said over and over that Cindy looked just like Cindy, which was her way of saying she looked like she'd remembered. Dawn, who'd been genuinely happy to see me a month ago, was beyond happy to see Cindy, who she'd looked up to as a child, and who she had named her favorite doll after.

Smart phone pictures were shared, a funny story or two was told, and the understood-but-not-spoken sentiment of sorrow for what Charlotte had done to Cindy was expressed. Cindy spoke of her children's anxieties. Dawn spoke of her children's similar issues. It was a family thing, the way family shares struggles, and the way they share emergency medicines.

At the end of the hour, everyone hugged again. Dawn's grip on Cindy was tight and it was long. Six months ago, Cindy would have sworn this day would have never happened. Three months ago, she'd have been almost as certain. One month ago, the odds were still stacked in favor of her never seeing the woman who idolized her as a little girl. Now, a day after seeing her, they are texting.

My Dad plans on making a point of seeing Dawn next time he is in Gainesville. He plans on hugging her neck. She plans on crying when he does.

As for Cindy and me, we feel certain that Dawn will become a part of our lives. She has wild, red hair and bubbles with enthusiasm, passion and sweetness. She is just too easy to like to not want her as part of our lives.

I will always be grateful that Claire answered my email. This book likely wouldn't have been possible without her being willing to open up to me, to introduce me to Dawn, and to share the story of her life with Charlotte. She answered questions that no one else could. Her generosity allowed Cindy and I some final steps in our healing.

Several months later, my daughters enrolled in college near Gainesville, Georgia. On the weekend we moved them in, I introduced Jane, Rachel and Laura to Dawn. I told Dawn that she was welcomed to bring Claire too, but Claire was busy with Dawn's kids.

Everyone loved everyone that afternoon at the restaurant. Dawn loved Rachel, Laura and Jane and vice-versa. Jane later told me that she had been moved by the warmth and genuineness of Dawn. I had been mostly quiet at the sandwich shop, watching what would have once been a most bizarre meeting but now seemed kind of normal.

Besides my stepsister, Amy, Dawn – a Burns, for Heaven's sake – was becoming the one in whom I was going to turn to first to be the most-trusted friend and protector of the ones whom I cherish above all else, my kids.

A year ago, I'd have thought an early August snow in Georgia would be more likely than me viewing a Burns as a most-trusted protector of my daughters.

Two years ago, I'd never imagine Rachel leaving home and going off to college.

Not every story ends well, at least not on this side of eternity. I know that. You know that.

Mike and his family have moved on as best they could after losing Erin. But until they are reunited in heaven, Erin dying at 19 will never seem right or fair. Not to me and certainly not to Mike. We all have sorrows and losses and heartaches that do not, and will not, make sense to us.

That's why staying is essential, for me and for you.

The pull to leave, to quit and to disengage will reappear in my life. I know this about myself.

I choose to stay.

The enemy would like nothing more than to see me betray the name God has given me.

I choose to stay.

Some will leave me, perhaps most.

I choose to stay.

I'm no longer Little Bill, or the one needing to be tended for, or the one ripe for being bullied. And I have what it takes to stay, because of who He is and who He says I am.

God said:

Wendy's? You chose Wendy's for this moment? OK, I actually orchestrated that too. You remember the older lady who worked there, who kept coming over and joking with you all? The one who hollered out as you left, 'Don't wait so long to see each other again.' That was my idea. You are on this Earth to be relational. The more lives you invest in, the better. Same with Cindy. The more you invest in people's lives, the greater chance you will get hurt. I know that. But what did that visit do to the lives of Dawn, Claire, Dawn's children, the older employee at Wendy's? You'll see when we're together on the other side of eternity. What seemed so insignificant to you and to Cindy. It was anything but insignificant.

And as for the role Dawn now plays in your life, it too is part of the good that I'm still bringing from the decades of hurt.

I will stay with you, Bill. Always.

Chapter 23 –
Christmas 2014

"And the peace of God, which transcends all understanding, will guard your hearts and your minds in Christ Jesus." – Philippians 4:7

"See ya next Christmas, sporty. I'll make myself obvious." – The Deceiver

Cindy and her husband Pat got to our house Christmas Eve; my parents got here Christmas Day in time for lunch. For the first time in four years, we were all under one roof.

I've long yearned for normalcy and easy living. For most of my life, that is what I have coveted the most. I naively believed that nine families out of ten had it, and I wanted what they had. A good Christmas, with a good, happy family surrounding me, in my head, that was normalcy. Now I think maybe it's the exception.

The scriptures never promised anything about normalcy or peaceful routine. But Jesus often sought it out in His own life, alone or with the twelve disciples or with the inner-group of Peter, James and John. And I wanted that.

But those times were the precious exception in Jesus' life. And they are in ours. We have basically been guaranteed that we wouldn't know easy living – at least not for long.

But unlike most of the previous years, I approached this Christmas hoping, and expecting, a good time of togetherness. That expectation alone speaks of the miracle of my new normal.

Before 2014, I can't remember the last time that Christmas was pure joy at our house. Some of Rachel's most anxious episodes occurred between December 23 and December 26. And me being hyper-focused on Rachel, I of course noticed this "coincidence" after the second year, the first time it loosely could be called a trend.

I didn't mention it, of course. But she knew it, too. I was hoping she hadn't remembered that for several Christmases in a row, she had at least a minor episode. But that was wishful thinking.

"I hope I don't have a panic attack this year at Christmas," she said in 2012.

"Why would you think you would?" I asked, pretending I hadn't logged these panic attacks on my mental and emotional calendar.

"Because I've had them the last few Christmases?"

"Really? I remember last year, but more than that?"

"Yeah. It seems like it's a pattern."

There was no pretending that either of us didn't remember the previous Christmas. We had begun the process of switching one of her primary anxiety medicines that year, while she was out of school on break. Cymbalta had somewhat worked on the anxiety over the last year, but it had made her explosive, particularly with Jane and Laura, and even more impatient than normal. Moodiness was a possible side effect, Dr. Hunt said. We would just need to get her back on Prozac and then taper her off Cymbalta, because it could be hard to come off of.

Turned out, that was a bit of an understatement.

Instructions were for one capsule every other day for two weeks, while reintroducing Prozac slowly. It sounded right, appropriately cautious. But Rachel was nervous, jittery and shaky during those two weeks, taking us back to some of her worst days.

The first time she went three days without Cymbalta was Christmas day, 2011. That night, she had a panic attack that had every terrifying characteristic of a seizure. She ended up on our bedroom floor, shaking, not quite a full-blown epileptic attack, but not a simple trembling. She now says it was the scariest of the scary times for her, "flashing lights in my head, a war raging in my body, like a huge man was sitting on my chest." It cemented how crappy Christmas memories were for us.

The following two years were better, though she was still nervous and didn't feel well.

So I entered Christmas Eve 2014 hopeful, but cautiously so. And this time, it wasn't only Rachel I was worried about. I knew that this special time together with all our extended family for the first time would face opposition, and probably in new and unexpected ways.

I'd have to fight for it and enlist support. I called my pastor, Craig Bowler, who loves well and me a good bit. He agreed to pray more than usual and specifically. Stan, my best friend for 30 years, had my back as well, just like he'd done for decades. I'd had moments the previous months doubting the wisdom of writing this book and claiming my name, and I needed prayer for that as well. In anxious flashes, I was terror-struck by the audacity of announcing my secret identity to the world. The battle is fought in the spiritual realm, but it often wreaked havoc in my physical life. I needed the most prayer for that.

Satan would love to dispel this claim God has made on me, and my family, in writing *Staying*. Throughout writing, the enemy whispered lies and I wrote them down. So I have no doubt that as the book works its way into your hands, I'll be targeted more.

But recently, the Father reminded me of this: *"Yes, you can use prayer by your band of brothers. But do not forget that the enemy has already lost his power over you."*

He led me to this passage: "When I was dead in my sins, God made me alive with Christ.... And having disarmed the powers and authorities, he made a public spectacle of them, triumphing over them by the cross." (Colossians 3)

Armed with the truth that the enemy has no claim over me, or my story, and that I was covered in prayer, I pressed on, putting the final touches on the book and preparing for the holidays.

Christmas 2014 came peacefully with no visible anxiety in my house for the first time in many years.

"I could lie and tell you that it didn't enter my mind," Rachel said on Christmas afternoon. "But I didn't ever get anxious. So take that, Satan!"

I had hoped for something miraculous out of this reunion, but I didn't fully expect it to happen.

Turns out though that the normalcy itself was the miracle. It was a gift, the kind that I recognized clearly and gave huge thanks for, and with apologies to Jane and everyone else, was far better than anything I unwrapped Christmas morning.

Sometime around midafternoon, I walked to my bedroom for a minute of quiet. Within a couple of minutes, Cindy knocked on my door.

"Dad wants to drive out to see our old house on Beckett Drive. Do you want to go?"

"Are you kidding me?" This would be gold.

Five minutes later, I was buckling into the back of my dad's SUV. Cindy rode up front, next to Dad. Laura and I were in backseat.

I write about Laura sparsely in this book. And I think she understands why. But I imagine in some deep place within her psyche, she will wonder why I poured out myself in this way for Rachel and not for her. Laura and I didn't share the 11 years on the softball fields. I don't remember once having to lie on her floor at night so she could attempt to go to sleep. She didn't call home from school everyday with a whimper.

She demanded less of me, and thus she got less of me. Not less of my heart, but less of my attention and energy. But maybe attention and energy equals heart, at least to a teenage daughter. So maybe she did get less of my heart. I can't get those years back. I'll rely on love covering the multitude of my sins and ask for grace and mercy from Laura.

There is so much to love about Laura, and so much that deserves attention.

I went to every school play she was in, and she's fabulously gifted. I shared her outrage at the injustice of school politics. Emotionally, I felt connected to her at times in which friends were hard for her to find. I understood that kind of loneliness and betrayal – that kind of abandonment.

She had every ailment Rachel had, just in smaller, or at least less obvious, amounts. She felt anxious and scared and unsure of her place in the world. It just didn't define her. I appreciated that about her, and told her so on more than one occasion. She can sit behind the piano and figure out how to play a song before she gets up, she sings like Julie Andrews and owns the stage when she's on it.

Many an early evening, I'd be 100 yards down the street, shooting baskets in the neighbor's driveway, and I'd hear her singing from her bedroom. I'd smile, equal parts amused by the volume and amazed by the talent.

On this day, she was sitting next to me, armed with a video camera, eager to help her dad in any way she could – particularly to capture the moment on film.

"What made you want to go Beckett Drive, Dad?" I asked my father.

He glanced back at me. "Just wanted to see what kind of shape it was in."

I sensed something deeper at work and decided to press in a bit. "Good memories for ya?" I asked, clearly fishing.

He smiled. "They are very good. We had fun there." He was silent a moment. Then, "Bobby Mock, have you heard from him?"

I pictured Bobby's round face and guilty smile.

"Not in about 35 years," I said.

"And what was the name of the lifeguard at the pool?" he asked.

"Norma," Cindy said.

"Norma!"

Just like that, we were back in the late '70s reliving simple scenes from some of our best years. And we all remembered our parts. Though we'd established a deeper family bond with each other over the last year, more than any of us had ever known, our emotions stayed largely beneath the surface, much like they did before.

I didn't mind, though. The tumultuous road back to my childhood had finally been explored over the last year, with Cindy and Dad alongside. Dad had pulled the masks off the monsters while holding me close, and we'd experienced some things together that neither of us knew were around the corner. And God had held us particularly close during those times.

It seemed we'd all found some peaceful normalcy we longed for. Pushing for more emotional transparency in the SUV, on Christmas Day, would have tarnished it. Initially, I had wanted more of a deep, meaningful experience in traveling down memory lane again. But God already had in mind what it was that I really wanted.

Before the holidays, I had repeated one prayer: *Please let us have this time, God, and let us be well.*

The day came, and we were all well.

Mom and Dad headed back down south the day after Christmas. Cindy and Pat left two days later. Rachel and Laura were soon back at school.

I stayed with Jane. And life seemed about as normal as it had ever been.

And I sensed God smiling.

A Note on the Voices

I don't have any more of a direct pipeline to God than the next person. I do believe we all have a direct pipeline and that God speaks to us in various ways. Sometimes for me, it's through music, sometimes it's on the softball fields and sometimes it's through the counsel of other believers. He speaks to us through his written word, too.

I'm convinced God isn't the author of confusion or deception. Right the opposite. He wants me to know His voice as He speaks to my soul, my conscious. When I began writing, I didn't set out to include God's words at the end of each chapter. But I realized there were many questions I felt God shedding light on during the writing. *Where were you? What was up with this or that? What was your heart toward me in this situation? Why didn't you do more in that instance?*

I wrote almost in free form what I believed God was saying. Then, I took it back to Him in prayer to make sure I was hearing him right. What flowed from my heart to the page was what I heard God speaking to me through the process.

Much of the time, I was fighting another voice. Not audible, but still a voice. It whispered accusations and lies.

I didn't want to give this condemnation, shame and degradation much space, but there were times it was barely kept at bay. Sometimes, the lies would overwhelm me like a tidal wave.

I tell you this mainly to say you're not alone. Deceit is who the Liar is and what he has set out to do. He wanted me to believe I'd check out emotionally and spiritually. He wanted me to believe that is who I really am.

"You think He loves you? I'll give you this much: He loves you the way a father loves a son who sucks. You're the son who lets his father down and can never get his act together. He may have to love you but he surely doesn't like you. How could He? You know what you've said, what you've thought, what you've done."

He is really good at discouragement: *He'll call you a fraud. Lazy. A failure. He'll say no one cares about your story. He'll say your "friends" don't really care, You're wasting your time. He'll even try to convince you staying is nonsense; most people wish you'd leave. They don't need you and they'd walk out on you anyway. No one, no where likes you because you've wreaked plenty of havoc and made yourself unlikable.*

The fiery darts of his lies can cripple you. But the accusations, while always intimidating and on point, are actually hollow and weightless when you see them from a larger perspective. God has already made a public spectacle of the enemy of our souls once (Col. 2:15). And He's going to do it again.

Be still and listen for the voice of the Lord. Ask him to let you hear his voice. Then ask him again. And then again. With time, we can get to the place where the voice of God is as recognizable as that of our best friend. And the voice of the enemy? It won't leave us altogether. Not even close, actually. But his chatter will start sounding like what it really is – a lie, a temptation, a distortion of truth or a condemning accusation.

Calling them out for what they are disarms their hold on us.

Will you join me in that quest?

About The Author

For two decades, **WILLIAM SANDERS** was an award-winning and Pulitzer Prize-nominated writer and editor for various daily newspapers, including the Atlanta Journal-Constitution. His specialty was front-page, human-interest feature stories. During his newspaper career, he was cited for writing best feature stories, best sports stories and best news stories in Georgia and regionally. He has written magazine stories on PGA golfer Phil Mickelson and baseball great Hank Aaron. His writing style has been called conversational and intimate. William coached girls' softball for 11 years and considers those years on the softball fields as a place of ministry.

Read more from WILLIAM SANDERS at:
www.william-sanders.com

Follow **"William Sanders, Author"** on Facebook
Follow him on Twitter **@billsanders1965**

Made in the USA
Lexington, KY
10 July 2015